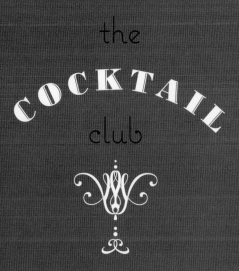

the

COCKTAIL

club

A Year of Recipes and Tips for Spirited Tasting Parties

MAUREEN CHRISTIAN-PETROSKY

Photographs by

THAYER ALLYSON GOWDY

Wardrobe & Prop Styling by Karen Schaupeter

Food Styling by Suzanne Lenzer

Abrams

NEW YORK

For Mom & Dad, whom I can't thank enough. You're amazing.

For Michael, my happiest hours are with you. All my love, always.

Published in 2014 by Abrams

Text copyright © 2014 Maureen Christian-Petrosky
Photographs copyright © 2014 Thayer Allyson Gowdy

Library of Congress Control Number: 2013945638

ISBN: 978-1-61769-026-6

Editor: Cristina Garces
Designer: Chin-Yee Lai
Production Manager: Tina Cameron

The text of this book was composed in Bodoni, Coquette, and Futura.

Printed and bound in China

10 9 8 7 6 5 4

Abrams books are available at special discounts when purchased in quantity for premiums and promotions as well as fundraising or educational use. Special editions can also be created to specification. For details, contact specialsales@abramsbooks.com or the address below.

TABLE of CONTENTS

INTRODUCTION

Good Drinks, Good Food, Good Friends: Join the Club

When I lived in Atlanta, my coworker, Sarah, started a book club. Results were mixed at first—some people really wanted to talk about the book, while others were just there to catch up. After I suggested we turn our monthly meetings into a wine club, our "book club" took on a life of its own. Work was where we had met, but wine club was where our friendship really grew. As adults, it's hard to find time to cultivate meaningful friendships. Wine club allowed each of us to rediscover friendship and network all while enjoying and learning about the best-tasting therapy around.

I graduated from the Culinary Institute of America and passed my sommelier certification with the Master Court of Sommeliers, but I learned more about wine in my living room than in any classroom lecture hall. That first wine club was the inspiration for my first book, *The Wine Club*. Although I've left Atlanta since the original wine club's inception, it's my latest wine club in my hometown of Bucks County, Pennsylvania, that inspired *The Cocktail Club*.

Amy, the liveliest and youngest member of my wine club, is twenty-nine years old and has five kids. She loves wine club (for obvious reasons), but it was a simple phone call from her that inspired me to get out of my wine world and start sipping cocktails. When it was her turn to host, she called me to get some ideas for fun cocktails to serve as guests arrived. We started with an Aperol Fizz, a spritzy little pour I had recently become fond of. After that, we kicked off every month with a cocktail. I loved looking for new ideas for that first sip of the night, and after lots of swirling and shaking, I'd found a new obsession that took my wine club in a whole different direction.

Throughout years of writing about wine, studying wine regions, and visiting wine-makers all over the world, there has always been some cocktail crossover. But never in a million years did I think my wine-loving heart would be craving a cocktail in lieu of my cherished wine. Although spirits were a part of my formal training, I am NO mixologist. Full disclosure: Before starting this cocktail club adventure, I was a total booze rookie. In fact, I had never really drunk "brown" booze! But at the end of the day, I couldn't resist the charming clink of the cubes, not to mention all of the stylish shakers that now dress up my bar.

Every year, our tastes change and our taste buds follow suit. Maybe you and your friends started off as beer lovers and progressed to wine, or perhaps you've always been into sipping scotch. Whether you like your adult beverages on the stiff side or prefer something sweeter, *The Cocktail Club* gives you a full year of excuses to get together each month with your friends to learn about the world of cocktails. It's like starting your very own speakeasy. No more lying about whether or not you read the book or scrounging around for *Cliff's Notes*; this club is all about enjoying yourself with the company of good friends. You'll learn there's a whole world outside of the classic Martini (though you'll get to try that, too!), but this book isn't about becoming a master mixologist or even a bartender—it's about finding out what cocktail suits you and having a great time doing it.

In the process of learning how to make great drinks, my friends and I have laughed our way to finding our own signature cocktails and favorite sips. Let's be honest: We all know that book clubs, investment clubs, knitting clubs —whatever you want to call the get-togethers—are the perfect excuse to socialize with friends, share a drink, and learn something along the way. So this year, join me and call it what it is: a cocktail club!

Getting Started, One Sip at a Time

Anyone can start a cocktail club. Novices and experts alike can follow along as we taste-test one type of base spirit or style of drink each month. Whether you're interested in entertaining tips or booze trivia, these pages have something for everyone. While I have created guidelines for running a club of your own, feel free to take them as you please. Along with the drinking, of course, you'll want something to snack on, so we've included recipes and snack ideas perfect for chefs or kitchen newbies. Nothing complicated here, just quick and easy hors d'oeuvres perfect for noshing alongside a cocktail. So get your drinking shoes on, it's time to kick off your cocktail club!

The Guest List

Once you mention a cocktail club, people will come out of the woodwork to join, but I recommend you keep each month's guest list to no more than ten people. We all love a good soirée, but the purpose of the club is to learn a little while enjoying those drinks, so keep your list limited. Also keep proximity in mind for safe travels at the end of the evening. If you live in a locale that allows members to take public transportation, then this factor doesn't come into play, but for clubs meeting in the suburbs, you can always call a cab, or simply take turns as the designated driver.

The Set-Up

There are literally thousands of cocktail recipes out there, but I've pared it down to the most popular, the classics, and some newcomer cocktails. Each month, you should choose your favorite four or five of the cocktails to taste test. Making these drinks is a big part of the experience, so I suggest you make at least one of the cocktails at your gathering each month to order and the others in bigger batches ahead of time so you still get to cozy up to the shakers, strainers, and other gadgets without being stuck playing bartender all evening. To begin, just sip and sniff during the first go-round, then once you each find your favorite, you can return to it for a full portion at the end.

Portion Control

So how exactly do you taste four or five cocktails each month and actually remember what you're learning about? It's all in the size of the pour. While each month's recipes make one standard-size cocktail serving, for the purposes of the club, each standard pour should be enough to serve three tasters. I recommend tasters be portioned out into shot glasses for ease of serving and sipping. Once you have taste-tested each recipe, club members are then welcome to shake, stir, whiz, or pour up a full-size serving to enjoy while discussing each month's spirit and cocktail tasting.

If you are keeping your guest list under ten, each snack recipe makes enough for guests to have one or two bites of each.

when it's your turn to host

All cocktail club members should be prepared to host at least one month's meeting. When it's your turn to host you should:

Plan Ahead If you plan on following the book for a year of cocktail club, choosing the same day and sticking to it (for example, the first Friday of the month) makes it easy for members to remember the date. When you are the host, send out a quick reminder a week in advance to get a head count.

Here is a checklist of things that you should have on hand when it's your turn to host:
- Water
- Pens and Cocktail Critique sheets (see page 11)
- Enough glassware for the number of guests attending, and smaller-sized shot glasses for the tastings
- Snacks (cooked, bought, or assigned to other members)
- A dump bucket for those who don't want to finish their tasters before moving on to the next cocktail. A bowl, pitcher, or empty vase will work in a pinch
- Ice. Make a few trays ahead of time and store the cubes in large zip-top bags until you need it, or pick up a bag or two before your guests arrive

Assign the Spirits & Snacks Some bottles are more expensive than others, so if a bottle is more than $20–$30, you may want to have guests chip in to split the cost. Assign snacks to other guests if you're not up for doing all the cooking.

Conduct the Meeting Typically, it is a good idea to have a buffer of time for guests to arrive and settle in. Then you can clink your glass and get it going. One of your roles as host is to walk your guests through the tasting. Make copies of the critique sheet on page 11 to take notes as you swirl, sniff, and judge each concoction as you go. It's normal that conversations will break off as the tasting progresses, so simply clink your glass again to bring your guests' attention back to the task at hand. Once you've tasted all the way through the cocktail line-up, your duties are done and you can join in on enjoying your favorite cocktail from the tasting.

Establish Ground Rules
- Be sure to have your designated driver or mode of safe transportation home in place before you start the evening. Leaving this task 'til late night will prove to be a bad idea.
- One-to-one rule: Make sure to drink one glass of water for each drink.
- Don't drink on empty. Always have a little nibble before you start taste-testing.
- Unless you are the designated driver, you must try all of the cocktails, even if it's just a teensy sip.
- You should wait until you have tasted and talked about each cocktail before pouring yourself a "real" drink (a full serving of your favorite sip from the night).
- You can serve your cocktails in any glass you have on hand, but try not to serve in ceramic mugs or paper cups to avoid lending off flavors to your drinks.
- Avoid perfumed lipstick, heavy perfume, or cologne in general.

the critique

Cocktail Critique Sheet:

Type of Base Alcohol:

Cocktail #.

Color:

Aroma:

Taste:

Body:

Finish:

First Impression/

Overall Notes:

- *Color.* What color is your drink? Is it appealing to look at?
- *Aroma.* Similar to wine-tasting, swirling and sniffing your spirits will lead you to all sorts of different aromas. Try to identify herbs and spices, fruits, and flowers.
- *Taste.* Often your drink will taste the way it smells, but sometimes bitter or sweet flavors may surface once it hits your tongue.
- *Body.* This is also called "mouthfeel," and it's exactly that—how it feels in your mouth. Is it crisp and refreshing? Smooth or cloying? Cocktails can range from light-bodied and austere to rich and full-bodied.
- *Finish.* Does the drink linger in your mouth (a long finish), or is it gone immediately after you swallow (a short finish)? Are the flavors that stick around pleasing or harsh?
- *First Impression/Overall Notes.* Do you like it or not? Is it appealing to the eye? Would you drink it again? Sometimes two or three sips are needed for your palate to adjust to new flavors, so don't judge on the very first sip.

the initial investment

Through sheer trial and error, I've found that so much of what makes a great cocktail is often the fun accoutrements that grace the glass. While you don't need anything extravagant to get started, here's a list of items you may want to purchase for a well-stocked bar:

The Essential Ingredients

- Bitters. Angostura definitely, Peychaud's if you're ready to branch out
- Club soda or seltzer water
- Fresh lemons, limes, and oranges and other garnishes, such as maraschino cherries and olives. See the Garnish Guide on page 13 for how to prepare them
- Ice, cubed and crushed
- Mixers. Ginger ale and an assortment of juices are good to start. See page 15 for tips on making your own mixers
- Simple syrup (see recipe on page 15)
- Triple sec or Cointreau
- Vermouth, both sweet and dry

- A cocktail shaker. This is the first piece of equipment you should acquire, so if you haven't already, be sure to grab one (or a couple) before it's your turn to host. To make your own out of two pint glasses, use a large glass with a wider mouth and a slightly smaller glass that the larger glass can fit over top of when inverted.
- Bar gear. There are many fun and functional bar builders out there. Some of my favorite go-tos are: wine opener, zester, paring knife, muddler, Microplane grater, jigger, strainer, cocktail spoon, swizzle sticks, citrus juicer, absinthe spoon, cutting board, Boston shaker, peeler, and pour spouts.
- Glassware. An assortment of tall (highball or Collins) glasses, short (rocks) glasses, and champagne flutes are fine to get you started. The glass makes a difference in how you experience a drink's flavors and aromas, and, lucky for us, an assortment of reasonably priced barware is now available in most home stores. I like the look of mismatched glasses, so I pick up odd glasses from yard sales, the Salvation Army, or vintage shops so I always have a nice assortment on hand. If you're stuck without the appropriate number of glasses, call it BYOG and have your friends bring their own.

A NOTE ON GLASSWARE CARE

While I love my dishwasher, I always wash and dry my glasses by hand. Dishwashers can leave behind soap, which may cause funky aromas. In the case of spritzy drinks such as beer, Champagne, and sparkling wine, residual soap can also reduce the bubbles, thus reducing the body.

Adequate drying is also important. Glasses that have been through a dishwasher can come out streaky or spotty due to air drying. It's a total bummer to be served a drink in a seemingly dirty glass. Using a dishtowel to dry your glasses might leave lint or off aromas in your glass, so stay on the safe side and stick to lint-free options like paper towels for perfectly polished glassware.

the techniques

These are the basic techniques you'll need to know to whip up the cocktails for each month ahead:

Stirring: Usually drinks composed of only spirits just require a stir. Stir gently for a few seconds, keeping an eye on the outside of the glass or shaker. Once it's frosted, you're finished.

Muddling: Any fruit or herb that is to be muddled should be washed first. To muddle, add a small amount of simple syrup or your spirit to your fruit or herbs in a glass. Then press lightly with a spoon or muddler to release the ingredient's aromas and flavors.

Shaking: You can shake with or without ice (dry shake). If you are shaking with ice, be sure not to overdo it—you are looking to chill the drink and slightly dilute it, not water it down completely. The key to the shaker is to give it about five good shakes. Keep an eye on the outside of your shaker; once it is frosty you are finished shaking.

Stirring	Muddling	Shaking

Floating/Layering: To successfully float an ingredient, it is helpful to use a spoon, preferably a flat bar spoon. Gently pour the liquid over the back of the spoon and let it slowly disperse or float on top of your other cocktail ingredients. If you just pour straight from the bottle, the ingredient's weight and speed of the pour may prevent it from floating, causing it to sink.

garnish guide

There are a few basic garnish cuts that we'll be using throughout the year. From left are washed and picked herbs for muddling or garnish, lemon slices or wheels, orange peels for twists, and lime wedges.

ᴖ The At-Home Mixologist ꙮ

Since cocktail creations are so much more than slinging drinks, bartenders have become "mixologists" much the same way that cooks have become "chefs." This book has no intention of teaching you how to become a mixologist; it's simply here to help you navigate from top shelf to your shelf. If you like to dabble in the realm of DIY, here are some key how-to recipes for you to add homemade mix-ins to your bar repertoire.

how-to
INFUSE YOUR OWN SPIRITS

The hardest part of making your own flavored or infused spirit is choosing which flavor you'd like. After that, it's a very simple and fun little DIY all your cocktail-loving friends will enjoy.

First, start with a neutral vodka, rum, or silver tequila. Stronger alcohol draws out flavors faster, so in this case you want the highest proof you can find. If you can actually get something higher than 80 proof, you should tame the heat by adding water after you're all finished infusing. The easiest place to start looking for flavors is with fresh herbs or vegetables like peppers, fennel, and cucumber. You can also use fresh fruit, but be sure it is ripe, not overripe. Some tips for infusing 2 cups (480 ml) of alcohol:

- *Hot peppers should be diced and seeded first; start with ¼ cup (60 g)*
- *Dried peppers are best soaked whole; start with ¼ cup (60 g)*
- *Avoid fine powders like ground cumin or cinnamon because they will make your infusion cloudy*

- *Take fresh herbs off their stems to avoid bitterness, about 6 sprigs*
- *Split vanilla beans lengthwise; 1 split bean is good*
- *Wash and leave berries whole; ¾ cup (175 g)*

First, choose a clean, airtight jar (mason jars are great for this). Wash your ingredients, if needed, and add them to the jar, fill it with about 2 cups (480 ml) of the neutral spirit, and put the lid on.

Place your infusion in a cool, dark place such as a cabinet or a closet. Don't place your jar on a heater, on top of your fridge (because the motor can cause that spot to run warm), or in the sun. Gently shake and test the mixture every day. In somewhere between 3 days and 1 week, you'll achieve the flavor you're after and know when to finish it. If you begin to taste bitterness, you'll know you went too far. Bitterness will only increase the longer your mix infuses, which is exactly why you are starting with only 2 cups (480 ml)—you can always start over without too much loss! Trial and error is the only way to learn what works best for your taste buds.

Once you've achieved your desired flavor, you should remove any large pieces of flavoring and then strain your infused spirit through cheesecloth or a coffee filter. You can either enjoy your creation right away, or store it as you would any other spirit.

how-to
MAKE YOUR OWN MIXERS

Store-bought mixers are laden with artificial flavors, sweeteners, colorings, and weird preservatives to make them shelf stable, so instead of waking up your cocktails, they drag them down. Homemade mixers instead lend fresh, bright flavors to your drinks.

SOUR MIX
MAKES ABOUT 4 CUPS (960 ML)

1½ cups (300 g) sugar
1 cup (240 ml) lemon juice, freshly squeezed and strained

1 cup (240 ml) lime juice, freshly squeezed and strained

The key to this recipe is to balance the sweet and sour components. In a small pot, heat 1½ cups (360 ml) water and the sugar until the sugar dissolves completely. Remove it from the heat and let the simple syrup cool until it reaches room temperature.

Add the citrus juices and stir until they are evenly combined. Use immediately or store the mix in the refrigerator until needed. It will last for up to 1 month. Try putting your own spin on this by using different citrus flavors like orange or pink grapefruit.

GRENADINE
MAKES ABOUT 1 CUP (240 ML)

¾ cup (180 ml) pomegranate juice
¼ cup (60 ml) simple syrup (recipe below)

2 to 3 drops of orange flower water (optional)

Grenadine is a pomegranate-flavored syrup used in everything from Shirley Temples to the Singapore Sling. Put the juice, syrup, and flower water (if using) in a container and shake. It will last in a sealed container in the refrigerator for 2 weeks. If you substitute ¼ cup (60 ml) of the pomegranate juice with ¼ cup (60 ml) of PAMA liqueur, it will last for up to 6 weeks in the refrigerator.

SIMPLE SYRUP
MAKES ABOUT 1⅓ CUPS (320 ML)

1 cup (200 g) sugar

1 (240 ml) cup water

In a small pot over medium-high heat, bring the sugar and water to a simmer and stir until all of the sugar has dissolved. If you are going to infuse it with fresh herbs or other flavorings, add those ingredients before you simmer, then remove or strain them out once the sugar syrup cools. This will last for 3 weeks in the refrigerator.

how-to
MAKE YOUR OWN BITTERS

MAKES ABOUT 2 CUPS (480 ML)

Not necessarily bitter in taste, bitters are more like a bartender's salt and pepper, used to season your drinks. Today it's not unheard of for bars to carry several flavors, and the real enthusiasts are making their own. Making your own bitters is sure to add to any cook's or cocktail enthusiast's repertoire.

The process of making your own bitters isn't hard, but tracking down some of the ingredients may prove difficult. There are three parts that you'll need: the bittering agents, like herbs, roots, or botanicals (these are easily found online); the agent that provides your main flavor; and the base spirit. Just as when you are infusing your own alcohol on page 14, using a higher-proof base spirit will speed up the process. High-proof vodka, bourbon, tequila, or rum will all work when making your own bitters, though their respective flavors will alter your final outcome.

Making bitters can take up to a month from start to finish. This recipe is a good base recipe that I've adapted from the bitters expert, Brad Thomas Parsons. You can finesse this basic recipe to add your own favorite flavors like root beer, coffee, or grapefruit.

2 tablespoons dried orange peel
Zest of 1 orange, sliced into strips
¼ cup (42 g) dried cherries
5 green cardamom pods, cracked
2 cinnamon sticks
1 whole star anise
1 vanilla bean, split lengthwise and
    scraped out (keep both the pod
    and the seeds)

¼ teaspoon whole cloves
¼ teaspoon cinchona bark
½ teaspoon cassia chips
2 cups (480 ml) rye whiskey
2 tablespoons rich syrup (1 part water plus
    2 parts turbinado sugar, heated until
    sugar has dissolved and cooled to room
    temperature)

Put all of the ingredients except the rye whiskey and rich syrup into a large mason jar and pour in the rye to cover. Place a tight-fitting lid on your jar and put it away in a cool dark spot for two weeks. Shake your jar daily.

Strain the liquid through cheesecloth or a coffee filter into a clean jar. Cover this new jar and set aside.

Place the solids in a small saucepan and cover with 1 cup (240 ml) of water. Bring to a boil. Lower to a simmer, cover the saucepan, and cook on low for 10 minutes. Remove from the heat and cool. Once this is cool, add to a second clean jar, cover, and store in a cool dark place for 1 week, shaking daily.

Strain the liquid in the second jar (discording the solids) and combine this liquid with the original rye mixture. Add the rich syrup and cover and shake to combine evenly. Keep at room temperature for 3 days. After 3 days, skim the top of any debris and strain once more through cheesecloth or a coffee filter and use in your favorite drinks.

You can fill smaller jars and gift to friends or keep it all for your home bar. This will last indefinitely, but it's at its best in the first year.

DIFFERENCE BETWEEN TINCTURES AND BITTERS

While both bitters and tinctures are used sparingly to boost flavor or add a different dimension of flavor to your cocktails, there's one main difference: Bitters are made from a combination of many flavorings and a tincture is made from a single flavoring. Bitters are also typically diluted with water or a sweetener, whereas tinctures have a very concentrated flavor at a much higher proof.

The Classic Martini, page 24

JANUARY

chapter 1

GIN

More To It Than Tonic— Though That Works Too!

What better way to kick off your cocktail club than with the most famous cocktail of all—the Martini! At the heart of this mix is gin, glorious gin. From the bathtub all the way to the glitz and glamour of Hollywood, this sip is well-loved by newbies and cocktail scenesters alike, making it a perfect pick for your first cocktail club meet-up.

Leave it to the Dutch to add finesse to the distillation process (that's what they call making a liquid into an alcoholic beverage) creating a spirit perfectly suited for sipping, stirring, and shaking with all sorts of delicious partners or enjoying straight up on its own. Rich in history, gin is a cocktail-menu staple, with concoctions ranging from serious drinks, like Martinis and Negronis, to fruitier sips like the Singapore Sling. Once primarily used as medicine to cure everything from belly aches to kidney problems, today it's used as a cure-all for creative blocks, broken hearts, and sullen men and women around the world.

The Gist of Gin

To help you find your way around gin, it's helpful to understand the different styles you'll find hanging around the shelves of your liquor store. Traditionally, gin is a neutral grain spirit flavored with juniper berries, but modern gin can include everything from orange peel to

almonds. These plant, fruit, and herb add-ins are often referred to in booze circles as "botanicals." In the beginning, it might be hard to smell and taste past the alcohol fumes, but once you get the hang of it, you'll be able to identify lots of different aromas.

Modern gins can include spices such as cardamom and nutmeg as well as any of these botanicals: juniper berries, almond, apple, black currant, lemon peel, orange, angelica, licorice, lavender, and cassia bark (cinnamon).

As with every spirit we'll explore this year, there's more than just one style of gin, and the only way to learn the difference is to taste them side by side. Like winemakers, distillers each put their own signature spin on their spirits, so there are always little differences from brand to brand. Here's a guide to the most popular terms you may come across on labels while shopping:

London Dry Gin When you order a gin cocktail, expect to get London dry in your glass. "Dry" implies that it is not sweet. London dry is what's considered the typical English style, where the botanicals are distilled right into the gin, not added later. This creates a light and aromatic flavor, making this the perfect pick for cocktails. One other note: Gin in this style can come from all over the world; it doesn't have to come from London! When you're out shopping, some popular brands you'll find are: Beefeater, Bombay and Bombay Sapphire, Classic Tanqueray, Tanqueray 10, Van Gogh, Boodles, Gilbey's, Old Raj, Citadelle, and Magellan.

Old Tom Gin This is known as old-style gin and tends to be a little sweet. Once wildly popular, this type of gin may be difficult to locate now, as dry gins tend to be more pleasing to our modern palates. Call ahead to your local store before going on a wild gin chase. Famous brands include Hayman's and Ransom.

Plymouth Gin Just as Champagne can only legally come from Champagne, France, British law stipulates that Plymouth gin can only be produced in the city of Plymouth. Its flavors are similar to London dry gin, but amped up—Plymouth has more body, and more variety in aromas that can range from fruity to citrusy. It's also very dry. The only brand is simply Plymouth Gin.

Holland Gin or Genever Known as Dutch style, this has an uber-junipery finish. Like England's Old Tom gin, genever is distilled from malted grain, giving it a slight yellow tinge. While London dry is more similar to vodka, this style is more in line with a very light whiskey. In this category there are subcategories, including the *jonge genever*, which is a light-bodied young gin that contains more grain than malt wine, and *korenwijn*, which is wood aged.

Because genever, or Holland gins, are big on flavor, they're best served neat or on ice, as their flavors can be tricky when mixed in cocktails. This type is harder to find, but brands like Bols, Bokma, De Kuyper, and Anchor Genevieve are available.

Modern or New Western Gins In order to compete with the vodka craze of the eighties and nineties, some gin distillers started to mimic that style of aroma-free, neutral spirits. As the cocktail culture continues to boom, new styles of "botanical" driven gins are re-emerging. These gins tend to have a more subtle flavor profile with a balanced botanical palate of flavors like vanilla and lavender, as opposed to the classic heavily juniper-flavored pours. Still made from neutral spirits, these gins are not necessarily grain based, and can include an array of flavorings from the area in which they are distilled. For example, Greyling Modern Dry Gin from Michigan uses local lavender. Other examples include Beefeater Wet, which is pear flavored; Hendrick's from Scotland, which features rose petals and cucumbers; and the creamy full-bodied American Aviation gin made with cardamom, lavender, Indian sarsaparilla, and anise.

What is Vermouth?

As you break into the world of cocktail making, you'll quickly see that bottles of both sweet and dry vermouth (pronounced ver-Mooth) are must-haves for your home bar. Vermouth is a fortified (meaning an alcohol like cognac or brandy is added) red or white wine that is flavored with botanicals. There are two main types, sweet or dry, but new lesser-known types like bianco, amber, and rose have been popping up on drink menus lately. Vermouth, like wine, is perishable. It used to have a bad rap in the states because we really didn't know what to do with it. Now we know that vermouth is surprisingly versatile, either sipped on its own as a delicate aperitif in the European style, or mixed up in cocktails.

Dry Vermouth is clear, bitter, and light-bodied, and is used to make the classic martini. Either the French brand Noilly Prat, considered the traditional pour, or the popular Italian Martini & Rossi are suitable for this drink. You may also find Gallo, Dolin, or Cinzano on the shelves.

Sweet Vermouth Typically a ruddy red color, this type of vermouth is full-bodied and sweetened with sugar syrup. You'd use this for cocktails like the Negroni or the Manhattan. The brands Noilly Prat, Dolin, and Martini & Rossi all make quality sweet vermouth.

NEW YEAR'S RESOLUTIONS

You're already off to a great start by kicking off your cocktail club this year. In case you needed a few more resolutions to add to the list, here are some that will make this year of drinking with friends even more fun.

- Don't judge a drink by its color. You may just find this year that you love bourbon instead of Cosmos.
- Be open-minded! Don't let labels, price, or reputation prohibit you from finding out what you really love to sip.
- Keep it simple. Hosting cocktail club should be just as fun as attending, so no need to go overboard on décor or fancy food—remember it's a club, not a competition.

The History of the Martini

Like most historical successes, the Martini's start is much disputed, with multiple sources claiming to be responsible for its creation. Feel free to choose whichever incarnation you like best, as long, of course, as you are pondering this over a nice cold martini.

There is an English claim to the cocktail dating back to the late 1800s, which pins its name to the famous firearm favored by the royal navy, called a Martini-Henry rifle. One was likened to the other because, allegedly, they both had a kick (though even English friends of mine believe the Martini cocktail was created in America, and they take their gin seriously).

Stateside, we have a few tales, too. Some say it was invented in the town of Martinez, California, by a bartender named Richelieu. In another story, the famed San Francisco "Professor" Jerry Thomas of the Occidental Hotel claimed he had created it for a miner headed to the town of Martinez.

On the other side of the country, New York's Knickerbocker hotel maintains that their bartender, Martini di Arma di Traggi, stirred it up in 1910 as a "Gin and French." Martini's method involved stirring his drink with lots of ice, straining it, and topping the whole thing with a lemon twist. It was his loyal bar patrons who are credited with changing the garnish to an olive, creating what we now consider the classic Martini cocktail.

Taste Test

There are two schools of thought for chilling your gin. One believes that if you chill your gin before serving it, say by storing it in the freezer, you won't dilute it with melted ice. The other proclaims that the flavor of the gin botanicals can actually be improved with a bit of dilution. The outcome: your first cocktail club taste test! Pour 1 ounce of gin (your choice) over ice to chill, and 1 ounce of the same gin that has been in the freezer for at least half an hour. Add one more pour of room temperature gin and smell them side by side and taste each. Can you tell the difference? Are any aromas present in one glass and not the other?

Often spirits, even wines, that are served well chilled (say, straight from the fridge or freezer) are considered "closed," which means that the aromas and flavors are harder to detect because the cold temperature muffles them. As they become warmer, they open up and it's easier to identify aromas and flavors. The reason why alcohol is often served very cold is because chilling the spirit changes the mouthfeel and stifles the burn from the alcohol, presenting a sip that goes down much more smoothly.

Is That An Egg in Your Cocktail?

Maybe you're more of an adventurous imbiber, but for most, the idea of using raw eggs in cocktails may be intimidating. Aside from the common eggnog, there are whole categories of drinks containing this lovely little protein. Along with the nogs there are fizzes—like this month's Sloe Gin Fizz (page 24)—sours, and flips. Sours and Fizzes can be made with or without the egg and typically they call for just the egg white. With Nogs and Flips, you get the whole egg or the egg yolk.

Including a whole raw egg, or even just the yolk or white, in your shaker creates a frothy top to your sip and a sultry feel as soon as it hits your mouth. If you like a creamy dreamy cocktail, you may just fall for an egg in your shaker.

SHAKEN OR STIRRED?

This simple sleight of hand has been cause for many a bar brawl. *The Savoy Cocktail Book,* considered a bible among drink fans, insists the Martini be shaken, although it was Bond, James Bond, whose famous "shaken, not stirred" line garnered attention for this team. On the flip side, Martini purists insist this drink be stirred, preventing the Martini from being overdiluted by melting ice, which is a direct result of being shaken.

❧ Get Your Drink On! ❧

Now it's time we jump into gin. Things to look for as you pour: First, be sure there are no foreign particles floating in your spirits. Gin should be crystal clear and free of any color, except if you are pouring up the bright blue Magellan gin. Some common aromas you'll find as you swirl include juniper, pine, eucalyptus, citrus peel, and even spices such as anise and clove. Remember to pay attention to how it feels in your mouth (the body) and if the finish leaves you wanting another sip.

From the smooth and elegant Martini and Negroni to the fun Sloe Gin Fizz and Grapefruit Gimlet Salty Dog, you're in for an unforgettable tasting.

Tips for This Month
All of this month's recipes are made with London Dry or American gins unless otherwise noted.

It's All in the Glass
For your tasters, be sure to have lots of shot glasses or smaller serving glasses. Make sure to have martini glasses, Collins or highball glasses, and old-fashioned or short glasses too, for the time when everyone decides on their favorite cocktail.

❧ The Classics ☙

THE CLASSIC MARTINI

SERVES 1

The original Martini recipe called for half London dry gin, half Noilly Prat dry French vermouth, and a dash of orange bitters, but the modern Martini is much drier. Some people swear by the vodka martini, but gin has and will always be the quintessential pour for this cocktail.

Ice cubes
1/4 cup (60 ml) gin

1 tablespoon dry vermouth
Lemon twist or olive, for garnish

In a mixing glass or shaker filled with ice, stir the gin and vermouth until your shaker becomes frosty on the outside.

Strain into a chilled martini glass and garnish. If you're going for the lemon peel garnish, run the outside of the peel (the yellow side) around the rim of the glass and then twist it, expressing the bitter oil into the gin, and drop it into the glass. Conversely, if you are going with an olive, just gently add it to the glass before you add your gin.

Note: For a dry Martini, reduce the vermouth to 1/2 ounce.

SHAKE IT UP

Swap your olive for a cocktail onion and you've got a Gibson.

SLOE GIN FIZZ

SERVES 1

Sloe gin is not a brand, but rather a type of gin made from infusing ripe wild sloe berries in gin, along with some sugar, resulting in a rich, tart sip.

Ice cubes
1/4 cup (60 ml) sloe gin
1 1/2 tablespoons freshly squeezed
    lemon juice

1 ounce simple syrup (page 15)
3 to 4 ounces (90 to 120 ml) club soda
Orange slice and cherry, for garnish
    (optional)

In a cocktail shaker filled with ice, combine the sloe gin, lemon juice, and simple syrup. Shake and strain them into a Collins or highball glass. Top with the club soda and garnish with the orange slice and cherry, if desired.

TOM COLLINS

SERVES 1

This drink is so posh, it has its own glassware, also known as a highball or tall glass.

Ice cubes
¼ cup (60 ml) London dry gin
1 tablespoon freshly squeezed lemon juice
1 teaspoon superfine sugar, or ½ teaspoons

simple syrup (page 15)
Club soda
Lemon wheel, for garnish

In a Collins glass or any tall glass filled with ice, add the gin, lemon juice, and sugar. Stir and top with club soda. Garnish with the lemon wheel and, if you're feeling fancy, serve with a swizzle stick.

SHAKE IT UP

By tweaking just one ingredient or instruction, you can create a whole new cocktail. Here are some of the popular gin spins using the same ingredients as the Tom Collins:
• Gin Fizz: Shake all of the ingredients together with the ice, then pour into a glass with no ice.
• Silver Fizz: Add an egg white and shake.
• Golden Fizz: Add an egg yolk and shake.
• Royal Gin Fizz: Substitute Champagne for the club soda.

CLASSIC GIMLET

SERVES 1

Talk about medicinal—this drink was conceived to fight off scurvy. The gin and lime juice combination was named the *gimlet* after the tool sailors used to tap into lime juice kegs onboard. The key ingredient here is Rose's lime juice (you can find it at almost any grocery or liquor store), and the classic recipe from the Savoy hotel bar is half gin to half Rose's. If you can't find it, you can substitute fresh lime juice and add a teaspoon of sugar or simple syrup.

Ice cubes
1¼ ounces gin

1¼ ounces Rose's lime juice
Lime wedge, for garnish

Stir the gin and Rose's lime juice in a shaker full of ice. Strain them into a chilled cocktail glass. Squeeze in a wedge of lime and serve.

THE NEGRONI

SERVES 1

This is one of my favorite cocktails, boasting a rich ruby red hue that's perfect for toasting with friends.

Ice cubes
1 ounce gin
1 ounce Campari
1 ounce sweet vermouth

2 to 3 ounces (60 to 90 ml) chilled
club soda (optional)
Orange slice, for garnish

In a cocktail shaker filled with ice, combine the gin, Campari, and vermouth. Shake and strain them into a rocks glass filled with ice and top with the club soda, if you choose. Garnish with an orange slice.

❡ New Twists ❡

GRAPEFRUIT GIMLET SALTY DOG

SERVES 1

I first tasted this lovely cold cocktail on a trip to the Greek isle of Mykonos with my brother. A salty dog is traditionally made with vodka, but here we substitute gin and add Rose's lime juice to create a gimlet-style salty dog. If you stick with vodka and skip the salt rim, you're drinking a Greyhound.

Lime wedge
Coarse salt, for rimming the glass
Ice cubes
¼ cup (60 ml) gin

1½ teaspoons Rose's lime juice
½ cup (120 ml) freshly squeezed
    grapefruit juice

Use the lime wedge to wet the rim of an old-fashioned glass. Lightly dip the rim in the salt. Fill the glass with ice and add the gin, Rose's lime juice, and grapefruit juice and stir.

❡ Eat Up! ❡

This month, our snacks play up the best gin has to offer. The cucumber kabobs are awesome alongside a Gimlet, while the goat cheese spread has a vibrant tang suited to nibbling alongside a solid chilled Martini. Our two types of bruschetta are suited to any of our cocktails, and sure to satisfy a healthy appetite.

CUCUMBER, MELON, AND MINT KEBABS WITH CHILI-LIME DIPPING SAUCE

SERVES 10 TO 12

½ honeydew melon, seeded
¼ cup (30 g) roasted peanuts, rough-
    chopped
½ cup (120 ml) sweet Thai chili sauce

2 tablespoons freshly squeezed lime juice
24 fresh mint leaves
1 cucumber, cut into ¼-inch (6-mm) slices

Using a melon baller, scoop the melon into 24 balls and set them aside.

In a separate small bowl, combine the chili sauce and the lime juice to make the dipping sauce. Sprinkle the chopped peanuts on top.

Using a long toothpick or short skewer, thread one mint leaf, one melon ball, and one slice of cucumber. Serve with the dipping sauce and chopped peanuts.

BRUSCHETTA TWO WAYS

1 baguette, about 22 inches (55 cm) long, sliced on the bias into ½- to ¾-inch (12-mm to 2-cm) slices

1 to 2 tablespoons olive oil

For the tuna and capers:

1 (5-ounce/140-g) can water-packed tuna, drained
2 tablespoons plus 2 teaspoons mayonnaise
½ lemon, juiced
1 tablespoon minced shallot or red onion

1 teaspoon olive oil
½ teaspoon grated lemon zest
Fresh ground pepper
1 tablespoon capers, roughly chopped

For the apple and cheddar:

1 large Granny Smith apple, cored and thinly sliced, skin on
½ lemon, juiced
6 ounces (170 g) aged yellow cheddar cheese, thinly sliced

1 to 2 tablespoons honey
Fresh ground pepper

Preheat the broiler and position a rack 5 to 6 inches (12 to 15 cm) from the broiler. Place the baguette slices on a baking sheet and brush them with the oil. Broil and toast them until golden, 2 to 3 minutes. (Times will vary as all broilers have different strengths, so keep an eye on them.)

Make the tuna and capers: In the bowl of a food processor, combine the tuna, mayonnaise, lemon juice, shallot, oil, zest, and pepper and pulse a few times until thoroughly combined. Top half of the toasted baguette slices with heaping teaspoons of tuna and sprinkle with a pinch of the capers.

Make the apple and cheddar: Toss the apple slices with the lemon juice to prevent them from browning. Place 1 to 2 slices of cheddar and 1 apple slice on each of the remaining baguette slices. Drizzle with honey and top with fresh-ground pepper.

GOAT CHEESE SPREAD

7 to 8 ounces (200 to 225 g) plain soft goat
   cheese, at room temperature
1½ tablespoons finely chopped fresh chives
2 teaspoons finely chopped fresh parsley
2 teaspoons finely grated lemon zest
2 teaspoons freshly squeezed lemon juice

½ teaspoon fresh cracked black pepper,
   plus more for garnish
Salt (optional)
1 or 2 crusty French baguettes
   (depending on size)

In a medium bowl, soften the cheese with the back of a wooden spoon. Add in the chives, parsley, lemon zest, and lemon juice and mix until evenly combined. Sprinkle on the pepper and season with a pinch of salt, if desired.

To serve, break off pieces of the bread and smear them with the goat cheese. Garnish with cracked pepper.

Note: Although I like to just rip pieces from the untoasted baguette, you can also slice and toast the bread in a 350°F (175°C) oven for 5 to 10 minutes.

10-Minute Happy Hour

Pressed for time but still want to have cocktail club this month? No worries—simply stick to a Martini tasting and an olive bar. Gather the ingredients for The Classic Martini (page 24), but buy two types of gin. Test the recipe using the two different gins and make a dry and classic version with each. Serve an array of different olives with crackers, and voilá—you've got your happy hour in ten minutes' time!

Adult Hot Chocolate with Toasted Marshmallows,
page 40

HOT COCKTAILS

Cocktail Club is Heating Up!

Get ready to taste this season's hottest cocktails—literally! The notion of hot cocktails may seem odd, especially if you reside in a sunny locale, but imbibers have been cuddling up with hot cocktails since fire was discovered. So if you've ever been frozen to your core, beaten down by the common cold, or just like to frequent ski lodges, you're sure to find a hot sip that suits you this month.

It's important to note that you're indulging in *hot* cocktails, so make sure to serve them steaming. Hot cocktails are not meant to burn the roof of your mouth, nor are they simply cocktails sans ice cubes. You want to create the perfect drink to cradle and sip slowly, so remember: Whether you're using a teapot to heat the water for your toddies or a Crock-Pot to make a big batch of spiked apple cider, steamy is the sweet spot for serving. That being said, you should be careful not to boil these, since boiling a cocktail will burn off the alcohol.

Though it may seem like something is missing without the charming clink of the cubes in your glass, I promise that hot cocktails are just as much fun to make and taste, and they're a perfect pour for this wintry month. So grab your heatproof glassware and get ready to get your hot drink on!

Not All Toddies Are Created Equal

If you've never had a hot toddy before, then you're in for a treat. In the cocktail world, not all toddies are the same. In fact, they're not even all hot! Back in the day, toddies always consisted of a spirit, sugar, water, and maybe grated nutmeg, with the addition of lemon and lemon peel by the end of the 1800s. Historically, the drink could be served hot or cold, and in the 1801 book *The American Herbal*, a toddy was cited as a healthy summertime sip (obviously not served steaming). Today, toddies come in many versions, but typically we reserve the term for hot sips.

According to cocktail guru David Wondrich, the traditional hot toddy is simply whiskey, sugar, and boiling water, with perhaps a bit of lemon peel. The toddy we'll taste this month is my take on the traditional, with a bit of fresh ginger thrown in to jazz up the original flavors. The addition of honey rather than sugar makes for a drink that isn't overly sweet and lets the rye whiskey shine. Hot toddies are best served from a big batch on the stovetop and, when done correctly, it is the ideal beverage to serve when the weather is cold or as a nightcap for a deep, comfy night's sleep. For centuries, the beverage at hand has been considered medicinal and in my household we still firmly believe a hot toddy will make you feel better than any cold or flu medicine you can buy. I've experimented with many versions and varieties, and my simple, soothing rye and ginger concoction (page 37) always does the trick.

PARTY FAVOR

When pouring any piping-hot boiling liquid into a glass (even if it claims to be heatproof), place a spoon in it first to prevent the glass from cracking. The spoon acts as a conductor, taking some of the heat from the glass.

❧ Get Your Drink On! ❧

When it comes to hot cocktails, you can't just add a shot to your coffee and expect to have a cocktail. Sipping hot drinks is fun, but keep in mind that these are still crafted drinks, so make sure to pay just as much attention to measurements and mixing instructions as you would with any cold cocktail.

This month, our hot sips range from stiff to sweet, including riffs on classics like the Rye and Ginger Hot Toddy (page 37) and new pours like the Hot Salted Caramel Cocktail (page 39). Or try a Hot Spiked Apple Cider, Mulled Wine, or Adult Hot Chocolate to see which cocktail style you like to sip on the steamy side.

Tips for This Month

It's All in the Glass

This month, you'll want to grab some mugs or heatproof glasses for our array of cocktails. When making an Irish Coffee specifically, it's ideal to have the correct stemmed coffee glass for the appropriate coffee-to-whiskey ratio. Regular mugs can be used in a pinch, but be sure to measure your coffee so you don't overpour it.

Keeping Cocktails Hot

Serving hot cocktails is a little trickier than cold cocktails because these sips need to be served steaming. Crock-Pots set on low are a great way to keep these drinks at the perfect temperature, so you may want to ask your fellow club members to bring theirs along for the evening.

Setting up drink stations will also make your cocktail club flow smoothly. Try setting up one or two cocktails in your kitchen, depending on your space limitations. Keep the teapot going for the Hot Toddies and another pot with a ladle for the Cider, Mulled Wine, or Hot Chocolate. If you're able to procure a Crock-Pot or two, set those up in a separate room, if possible, to prevent a back-up at the kitchen cocktail station (as well as to provide more opportunities for mingling!).

Spice It Up

In tales of cocktail lore, bar owners and tenders used to keep a spice box on hand for making hot toddies. Make your own box, including an assortment of whole spices such as cinnamon, nutmeg, cloves, and anise (I bet lots of your friends have never even seen a whole nutmeg!). You can store the spices loose and keep a small handheld grater with your bar couture for fresh grating if a cocktail calls for it, or you can make little pouches of your own personal bar spice blend with cheesecloth and twine.

The Classics

RYE AND GINGER HOT TODDY

SERVES 1

Rye whiskeys range from robust and spicy to smooth with vanilla and caramel flavors, making them the perfect pick for whipping up Hot Toddies. Substituting other spirits such as bourbon, Irish whiskey, or Scotch, will create different flavor profiles. If you want to try something different entirely, you can create a Hot Tea Toddy by using hot herbal or traditional black tea in place of the hot water.

2 to 3 thin slices fresh ginger, peeled
1½ ounces rye whiskey

2 teaspoons honey
Lemon wedge, about ⅛ of a lemon

Add the ginger to a teapot or saucepan containing 1 cup (240 ml) water at room temperature. Heat the water until the teapot whistles or your water starts steaming.

While the water heats, combine the whiskey and honey in a heatproof mug and squeeze in the juice of the lemon wedge. Strain the ginger-infused hot water into the mug. Stir to dissolve the honey and enjoy.

MULLED WINE

SERVES 10

I was never into the idea of hot wine, but I was won over this past Christmas when an offering of mulled wine turned out to be the beginning of the best party all season. Mulled wine is now officially in our holiday repertoire and will certainly pop up again throughout the winter. Typically, it includes a mix of hot red wine, sugar, spices, and sometimes brandy. If you are new to mulled wine or already a fan, you're sure to enjoy this spiced-up version with peppercorns and anise.

Two (750 ml) bottles fresh, good-quality
red wine
½ cup (240 ml) honey
Zest of 1 orange
Zest of 2 lemons

1 tablespoon peppercorns
3 whole star anise
3 cinnamon sticks
4 whole cloves

In a large pot or Crock-Pot, combine the ingredients and heat them on medium-low until they are steaming. Do not boil. Reduce the temperature to low, ladle the wine into mugs or heatproof glasses, and enjoy.

IRISH COFFEE

With a shot of Irish whiskey in their coffee, it's no wonder the Irish lads and lassies have been hollerin' "Top o' the mornin'!" Many variations of the Irish Coffee recipe exist, but in the most general of terms, you'll need some hot coffee, brown sugar, and the key ingredient—Irish whiskey—with some freshly whipped cream to top it all off. An important note: Any time you are serving hot coffee, hot cocoa, or hot tea cocktails, make it fresh. Don't try to pass off this morning's leftovers.

½ to ¾ cup (120 to 180 ml) hot, fresh-brewed coffee
1 teaspoon brown sugar

1½ ounces Irish whiskey
Freshly whipped cream (opposite)

Rinse your mug or glass with hot water first to take the chill off and prevent it from cracking. Fill your glass about three-quarters full with the coffee and add the sugar. Stir until all of the sugar is fully dissolved. Add the whiskey. Dollop the whipped cream on top and enjoy while hot!

SHAKE IT UP

Buena Vista Irish Coffee: Substitute the brown sugar with two white sugar cubes and lightly whip the cream, pouring it into the coffee over the back of a warmed spoon.
Bailey's Irish Coffee: Substitute all of the Irish whiskey with Bailey's. This version is sweeter and fuller-bodied than the traditional.
Mexican Coffee: Substitute the whiskey with half tequila and half Kahlúa.
The President's Coffee: Just in case you plan on toasting President's Day, substitute the whiskey with cherry brandy and whip the cream with a teaspoon of grenadine.

HOT BUTTERED RUM

These days, putting a pat of butter in your drink is kind of a faux pas, but even I can admit that, like anything with butter, this drink is pretty delicious. I like to add my own compound butter, incorporating the spices listed below to each glass, but you can just as easily add everything separately.

1 teaspoon soft unsalted butter
1 teaspoon dark brown sugar
1 pinch of freshly grated nutmeg
4 drops of vanilla extract

¼ cup (60 ml) dark rum
¼ cup (60 ml) boiling water
1 cinnamon stick

In a heatproof mug or glass, using the back of a spoon, mix the butter, sugar, nutmeg, and vanilla until evenly combined. Add the rum, boiling water, and cinnamon stick and stir to combine. Serve hot.

HOMEMADE WHIPPED CREAM

My childhood friend Christy's mother always had fresh whipped cream for her hot cocoa. To me, this was the ultimate indulgence and now, as an adult, hot cocktails topped with freshly whipped cream are the ultimate treat.

For this recipe, you can use an electric mixer fitted with a whisk attachment or a hand held whisk. You can alter the base flavor by adding an extract or alcohol of your choice ½ teaspoon at a time to each cup of cream while it is still liquid.

2 cups (480 ml) heavy whipping cream, cold
1 tablespoon powdered sugar, sifted, or more to taste

½ to 1 teaspoon flavoring (optional)

In a clean bowl, combine the cream, sugar, and flavoring if you'd like. Whisk until the mixture has tripled in size and can form soft peaks.

Note: If you have doubts, it's better to stop whipping the cream once you have achieved soft peaks (the peaks will softly fold over when the whisk is removed). You can always hand whisk a couple of times right before serving to bring the cream to stiff peaks (when the cream stands at attention) but you can't salvage overwhipped cream.

New Twists

HOT SALTED CARAMEL COCKTAIL

SERVES 1

¼ cup (60 ml) dark rum
1 tablespoon caramel sauce
1 teaspoon soft unsalted butter
4 drops vanilla extract

¼ cup (60ml) of boiling water
Freshly whipped cream (above)
Pinch of sea salt

Add the rum, caramel sauce, butter, vanilla, and water to a heatproof mug or glass and stir to combine. Finish it off with a dollop of freshly whipped cream and a sprinkle of sea salt.

SPIKED HOT APPLE CIDER

SERVES 1

½ cup (120 ml) apple cider
¼ cup (60 ml) whipped cream–flavored vodka

1 cinnamon stick
Freshly whipped cream (above)

Combine the cider, vodka, and cinnamon in a saucepan and stir over medium heat until they are warm. Serve in a heatproof mug or toddy glass with a dollop of whipped cream on top.

ADULT HOT CHOCOLATE
WITH TOASTED MARSHMALLOWS

SERVES 4 TO 6

4 cups (960 ml) whole milk
½ cup (100 g) sugar
⅓ cup (35 g) unsweetened cocoa powder
Pinch of salt

¾ cup (180 ml) marshmallow-flavored
* vodka*
4 to 6 large marshmallows, toasted
* (recipe follows)*

In a small saucepan over medium heat, combine the milk, sugar, cocoa, and salt. Stay nearby, as the milk can quickly boil over. Whisk it until smooth, creamy, and steaming.

Divide the cocoa among 4 to 6 heatproof cups, add 1 to 1½ ounces of the vodka to each, and stir to mix.

Toast marshmallows: Place marshmallows on a foil-lined baking sheet and brown marshmallows on all sides with a kitchen torch or under the broiler in your oven.

Top each hot cocoa with a toasted marshmallow and serve.

Eat Up!

When pairing treats with hot cocktails, it's best to keep it simple. Since our hot cocktails range from sweet to spicy, our snacks this month follow suit. The Chorizo and Nutella Bruschetta starts with the sweetness of the chocolaty hazelnut spread and finishes with a spicy kick from the chorizo, making it a great match with a Hot Toddy or a mug of Mulled Wine. Our Easy and Elegant Cheese Platter has salty, sweet, and savory all in one place, making a perfect snack for guests who like to graze and an ideal accompaniment to the Salted Caramel Cocktail or the Spiked Hot Apple Cider. The Simply Addictive Sugar and Spice Nuts work with every cocktail this month, enlivening the sweeter sips and complementing the zestier ones.

SIMPLY ADDICTIVE SUGAR AND SPICE NUTS

SERVES 12 TO 14

⅔ cup (130 g) granulated sugar
⅓ cup (65 g) packed dark brown sugar
1½ teaspoons kosher salt
1 teaspoon ground cinnamon
1 teaspoon roughly chopped fresh rosemary

¼ teaspoon cayenne pepper
1 large egg white
1 pound (455 g) walnuts, pecan halves,
   or almonds (or a combination)
½ cup (70 g) pine nuts

Preheat the oven to 300°F (150°C).

In a little bowl, combine the sugars, salt, cinnamon, rosemary, and cayenne.

In a large bowl, beat the egg white with 2 teaspoons of water until frothy. Add the nuts to the egg white and stir to coat evenly. Sprinkle them with the sugar mixture and toss until evenly coated.

Spread the sugared nuts in a single layer on a parchment-lined sheet pan and bake for 20 to 25 minutes, stirring occasionally, until golden brown and toasted. Remove them from the oven and separate the nuts as they cool.

Serve at room temperature or, once cooled, store in an airtight container for up to a week.

EASY AND ELEGANT CHEESE PLATTER

1 (4-inch/10-cm) wheel ripe Brie
About 6 ounces (170 g) blue cheese
About 7 ounces (200 g) smoked Gouda
About 8 ounces (225 g) Manchego
2 tablespoons cherry preserves
1 tablespoon honey

About 4 ounces (115 g) membrillo
 (quince paste)
1 bunch seedless red grapes
1 bunch seedless green grapes
½ cup (85 g) dried cherries
¾ cup (130 g) dried apricots
Breadsticks and/or crackers, for serving

On a large platter or wooden cutting board, place each of the four cheeses in separate corners. Remove a small wedge from the Brie; spoon the cherry preserves over the whole wheel and allow them to drizzle down the sides of the cheese. Drizzle the honey over the wedge of blue cheese and let a little bit pool on the platter or board. Place the membrillo near the Manchego.

Place each bunch of grapes at opposites sides with the stem ends facing the edge of the board or platter. Make sure the amount complements, not overwhelms, the cheeses.

Mound the dried cherries and apricots separately. Serve with breadsticks or crackers on the side. Use small knives and cut a few pieces from each cheese to get it started for your guests.

CHORIZO & NUTELLA BRUSCHETTA

SERVES 10 TO 12

½ slender baguette, cut on the bias into
 18 slices (½ to ¾ inch/12 mm to
 2 cm thick)

Nutella
1 6-inch link of dried chorizo sausage
 (see Note), sliced very thinly on the bias

Spread a little Nutella on each baguette slice and top with 2 to 3 slices of chorizo.

Note: Be careful to only buy Spanish chorizo and not Mexican. Spanish chorizo is a hard cured sausage that does not need to be cooked before eating, much like a pepperoni. Mexican chorizo is a fresh sausage and requires cooking before eating. If you can't find Spanish chorizo, you can substitute spicy pepperoni.

10-Minute Happy Hour

Have you ever heard the saying, "Apple pie without cheese is like a kiss without a squeeze"? New Englanders love apple pie topped with cheddar cheese, and this inspired combination of apples and cheese has been adopted around the world. If you don't have time to whip up four or five cocktails this month, channel this winning combination by whipping up a batch of Spiked Hot Apple Cider (page 39) paired with a platter of cheddar cheeses, breadsticks, and crackers for a quick and delicious happy hour.

Sidecar, page 50

MARCH

chapter 3

BRANDY

One Spirit, Multiple Personalities

This month, our star in the shaker is brandy and we'll be exploring her many personalities, from flirty applejack to serious cognac. We'll kick off the brandy experience with classics, like the savvy Sidecar and the fruity Singapore Sling, but we'll also shake things up with some newfangled takes sure to make your favorites list, like the Mason Jar Basil Pisco Sour and Brandy Alexander Ice Cream. Buckle up—it's time to get into all things brandy.

The Basics of Brandy

Brandy is the spirit that comes from distilling wine or any other fermented fruit juice. Between brandy and cognac, the distilled wine category can get a little confusing. Just like Champagne is a type of sparkling wine from Champagne, France, Cognac is a brandy from Cognac, France. From decadent Cognacs such as Hennessy, Rémy Martin, Louis Royer, or Courvoisier to delicious American brandies such as E&J, Christian Brothers, and Paul Masson, you've probably experienced this familiar sip at one point or another. In fact, even if you think you're not a brandy drinker, I can bet you've had it without knowing, especially if you've ever sipped sangria.

Brandy can get a little more complicated than other spirits, with its many labels and categories, so I've listed all of the subcategories below, each pouring up something unique and fun to sip. For this month's cocktail club, our recipes can be made with any of the American brands listed below, and you may also substitute cognac if you are, as my friend and colleague Mark Spivak says, "feeling flush, want to enhance your image, or are making a rap video."

Brandy 101

Eau de Vie French for "water of life," eau de vie is a distilled spirit made from most any fermented fruit except grapes (though there is a category called *eau de vie de vin*, which is made from grapes outside of the Cognac and Armagnac regions). Eau de vie is clear and colorless, is not aged in wood, and is usually served after dinner as a *digestif*. Its flavors are easily conveyed on its label. Completely apart from sipping, these typically fruity spirits all work exceptionally well when making desserts, especially anything involving chocolate! Popular eau de vie flavors include: *kirsch* or *kirschwasser* (cherry), *framboise* (raspberry), *mirabelle* (plum), *Poire Williams* (pear), and *pomme* (apple).

Cognac and Armagnac The best grape brandies in the world come from these two spots in southwest France, and these sips ring in from $20 a bottle to obscene prices at auction for aged and rare bottlings. Of the two, Cognac is definitely the more popular internationally, with Armagnac still struggling to gain its spot at the bar outside of France. You may notice these distinctions on their labels:

- **Three Star or V.S.** stands for Very Special and means it has been aged in oak barrels, typically from Limousin and Troncais, for at least two years.
- **V.S.O.P.** stands for Very Superior Old Pale; this gets a minimum of four years aging in oak.
- **X.O.** stands for Extra Old, and means it has been aging for at least six years, though this minimum is soon to be raised to ten years.

In the glass, Armagnac tends to be a little rough around the edges. It has a stronger flavor than Cognac and typically you wouldn't use it when a cocktail calls for brandy. It can be funky smelling, similar to that whiff of barnyard you can sometimes get from Burgundy wine, and it delivers a slight punch in the back of the throat—definitely an acquired taste. Both bring vanilla and caramel notes to the glass from their oak aging, but Cognac seems to do it more subtly than its aggressive cousin Armagnac.

Calvados Another French brandy, though this one is made from distilling fermented apple cider aged in Limousin oak barrels. Calvados is typically a light caramel color with apple flavors that range from crisp and tart to more ripe and juicy. You might also taste aromas of cinnamon and even butterscotch. This brandy is more rustic than Cognac or Armagnac, and works great in the kitchen in sauces and glazes.

Applejack This American brandy dates back to the Pilgrims, and in Colonial circles it was considered the in-crowd's drink of choice. Laird & Company, the most famous distillery located in New Jersey, cranks out delicious apple brandy with twenty pounds of apples jammed into each bottle. Applejack works well in all sorts of yummy cocktails, with the same appley good flavors and aromas as its French counterpart, Calvados.

Brandy de Jerez (Sherry) Like Cognac and Armagnac, this brandy can only be produced in the region it's named for—Jerez, Spain. Spanish brandies are big-boy drinks, considered more earthy than Cognac and range from lighter, nutty pours to complex sips with molasses, raisin, and burnt caramel notes. These are best saved for sipping on their own after a meal. *Solera* is aged an average of one year and is lighter and fruity, *Solera Reserva* is aged an average of three years in sherry casks, and *Solera Gran Reserva* is aged ten years or longer.

Pisco Whether Peruvian or Chilean, pisco ranges from clear with a slight yellow tinge to amber. Peruvian pisco is made in a pot still, and bottled in small batches. Due to the nature of this bottling, Peruvian pisco batches are more inconsistent than those pouring from Chile. Chilean pisco is produced with more modern techniques and in larger batches, so it tends to be lighter and brighter, making it easier to work into a variety of cocktails.

Taste Test

This month, set up a Pisco Sour taste test. Make one with a store-bought sour mix and one with sour from scratch (page 15). Take a sip and let your palate be the judge. Typically, store-bought sour is much sweeter and can leave a chemical aftertaste. So if sweeter sips are your preference, you're in luck with store-bought. If not, you're like me, and just added one more thing to your to-do list.

Grappa and Marc Sometimes called "poor man's brandies," marc, coming from France, and grappa, from Italy, both have their fans. Each are made from the leftovers of grapes (stems, skins, and such) that have been pressed for making wine. For our purposes, we won't be using any of these brandies in our cocktails, since we're looking to layer flavor and not simply to burn out our taste buds.

PARTY FAVOR

The Brandy Crusta is a classic brandy cocktail that includes maraschino liqueur, fresh lemon juice, Cointreau, bitters, and lemon peel. It is considered the first "fancy" cocktail. Around 1850, it was invented by Joseph Santini of one of the most posh bars of the time: The Jewel of the South, in New Orleans. The Brandy Crusta was the first to feature the "crust" on a goblet glass made by wetting the rim with a wedge of lemon and dipping it into sugar. Today, we can thank the Brandy Crusta for inspiring all sorts of fancy colors and flavors of sugar rimmers on the market.

❧ Get Your Drink On! ☙

Brandy cocktails run the gamut from lively and refreshing like the Pisco Sour, to rich and sweet like the Brandy Alexander. This month showcases its varied flavors, with new twists like adding basil to our Pisco Sour and showcasing the Brandy Alexander as an edible ice cream cocktail. If you're looking to sip a Cognac-based drink, go for the classic Sidecar; if fruity is your thing, you must shake up a Singapore Sling.

Tips for This Month
It's All in the Glass

Typically, if you're sipping brandy alone, it will be served in a snifter, which is a giant glass bowl with a tapered top. The glass has a large surface area for your hand to fit snugly around and warm the brandy, while the tapered top traps in the aromas for you to enjoy.

Since we're sipping cocktails this month, gather up the usual suspects of highball and old-fashioned glasses. You may also want to grab some mason jars from the grocery store—these do double duty as a shaker and as a serving vessel when making the traditional Pisco Sour (page 49) or the Mason Jar Basil Pisco Sour (page 51). Our Pear & Prosecco Cocktail (page 51) calls for champagne flutes, so if you choose this as one of your cocktails this month, have them at the ready.

❦ The Classics ❧

PISCO SOUR

SERVES 1

The traditional Pisco Sour includes an egg white. If you're squeamish about this, try the Mason Jar Basil Pisco Sour (page 51).

Ice cubes
¼ cup (60 ml) pisco
1 ounce freshly squeezed lemon juice

1 ounce simple syrup (page 15) or
* 1 teaspoon sugar*
1 small egg white
3 to 4 drops of Angostura bitters

In a cocktail shaker filled with ice, combine the pisco, lemon juice, simple syrup or sugar, and egg white and shake. Strain them into a chilled cocktail glass and add the bitters on top to finish.

THE SINGAPORE SLING

SERVES 1

The Sling—be it gin, whiskey, rye, or other—is usually a mix of sweetened spirits and water. These sips predate the cocktail era with the most famous version, the Singapore Sling, credited to Mr. Ngiam Tong Boon of Raffles Hotel in Singapore in the early 1900s still served there today. It's a frothy-topped, refreshing sip perfect for summer. Want to really re-create the Raffles experience? Serve up some roasted peanuts in the shell alongside your sling and, in Raffles Hotel Long Bar tradition, simply toss the shells on the floor.

Ice cubes
¼ cup (60 ml) gin
¼ cup (60 ml) pineapple juice
1½ tablespoons Cherry Heering or cherry
* brandy*
1½ tablespoons freshly squeezed lime juice
2 teaspoons Bénédictine liqueur

2 teaspoons Cointreau
2 dashes of grenadine (page 15)
1 dash of Angostura bitters
Club soda
Maraschino cherry, for garnish
Pineapple wedge, for garnish
Orange wheel or twist, for garnish

In a shaker full of ice, combine the gin, pineapple juice, Cherry Heering, lime juice, Bénédictine, Cointreau, grenadine, and bitters.

Shake and strain the mixture into a tall glass (highball or Collins) filled with ice. Top with a splash of club soda and garnish with the cherry, pineapple wedge, and orange wheel.

SIDECAR

SERVES 1

As with most recipes, there are many versions of this one floating around, but they all contain these three ingredients: Cognac, Cointreau, and fresh lemon juice. According to Mr. Ted Haigh, a.k.a. Dr. Cocktail, this is a "comfortably adjustable drink." Too sweet? Lessen the Cointreau. Too strong? Decrease the brandy. Too sour? Decrease the lemon juice. Here's the vintage version, but feel free to adjust to your taste once you've got this trio in place.

Ice cubes	Lemon wedge, optional
¼ cup (60 ml) Cognac	Sugar, for the rim, optional
1 ounce Cointreau	Flamed orange peel (recipe below; optional,
1 ounce freshly squeezed lemon juice	but it makes it more fun!)

In a cocktail shaker filled with ice, shake together the Cognac, Cointreau, and lemon juice.

Use the lemon wedge to rub around the rim of an old-fashioned glass, then lightly dip the rim in sugar, if you choose. Fill your glass with ice and strain the drink into the glass. Garnish with the flamed orange peel, if desired.

HOW TO MAKE A FLAMED ORANGE PEEL

The flamed orange (or lemon) peel is a bar trick sure to impress your guests. It's simple to make: Using a sharp paring knife, remove a piece of the peel from your citrus in a circular manner, starting at the middle and continuing all the way around the fruit. You only want the skin and the oils, so try to avoid as much of the pith (the white part) as possible since it can give your drink a very bitter taste. Using a match or a lighter, hold the flame over the glass. In your other hand, hold the twist skin-side facing away from you and gently squeeze the oils into the flame. The flame will burst out, so be careful not to have it facing directly at anyone. Once it lights, simply drop the peel into the glass.

New Twists

PEAR & PROSECCO COCKTAIL

SERVES 1

1 ounce Poire Williams eau de vie   3 ounces (90 ml) Prosecco, chilled

In a champagne flute, add the pear brandy and top it with the Prosecco.

MASON JAR BASIL PISCO SOUR

SERVES 1

Small mason jars are just about my favorite way to mix up drinks for a party. The jars create adorable individual shakers for premeasuring your ingredients. When your guests arrive, they can just add ice, any bubbly ingredients that may be called for, place the lid on, and shake. This way you aren't stuck at the bar mixing a multitude of drinks. Leave a bottle of club soda on the bar for guests who prefer their cocktails on the spritzy side.

Ice cubes
¼ cup (60 ml) Chilean pisco
1 ounce freshly squeezed lime juice
1 ounce simple syrup (page 15)

4 to 6 fresh basil leaves (twist or bruise
right before adding to the mason jar)
Club soda (optional)

In a mason jar or shaker filled with ice, add the pisco, lime juice, and simple syrup. Twist or bruise the basil leaves and drop them in. Put the lid on and shake.

Remove the lid and add a splash of soda, if you'd like, to finish. Strain into a glass and enjoy immediately.

❧ Eat Up! ❧

This month we have an easy and elegant Fig Flatbread with Parmesan—a great snack to pair with anything spritzy, including this month's Pear & Prosecco Cocktail (page 51). Also on the menu is a killer dish of Seared Scallops in Apple Brandy Cream Sauce, which is lovely alongside a Sidecar (page 50). We'll end our cocktail club with something sweet: The completely decadent Brandy Alexander Ice Cream. Go forth and indulge.

BRANDY ALEXANDER ICE CREAM

SERVES 6 TO 8

2 cups (480 ml) heavy cream
1 cup (240 ml) half-and-half
¾ cup (75 g) sugar
½ vanilla bean

6 large egg yolks
3 ounces (90 ml) brandy
¼ cup (60 ml) crème de cacao

In a heavy-bottomed saucepan, bring the cream, half-and-half, sugar, and vanilla bean to a boil.

Put the egg yolks in a large stainless-steel bowl. Add the hot cream mixture a little at a time while whisking continually, until the cream is completely incorporated. Pour the entire mixture back into the saucepan and heat it over medium-high heat for 1 more minute, stirring constantly. Remove it from the heat and strain the custard into a clean bowl. Add the brandy and crème de cacao and stir until they are evenly combined.

Cool the custard over an ice bath (a larger bowl full of ice and water) until it is cool to the touch. Freeze the custard in an ice cream machine according to the manufacturer's instructions. Pack it into a freezer-safe container and freeze.

This can be made up to a week in advance and stored in the freezer. Serve a small scoop in a coupe glass or a small dish.

SEARED SCALLOPS
WITH APPLE BRANDY CREAM SAUCE

SERVES 8

1 tablespoon extra-virgin olive oil
1 tablespoon minced shallots
¼ cup (60 ml) Calvados
½ cup (120 ml) heavy whipping cream
8 large sea scallops, patted dry
Salt and fresh ground pepper

Vegetable oil, for searing
¼ cup (60 ml) fresh unfiltered apple juice
 (see Note)
1 large clove garlic, minced
5 ounces (140 g) fresh spinach leaves

Heat ½ tablespoon of the olive oil in a large nonstick skillet over medium-high heat. Add the shallots and stir for 30 seconds. Add the Calvados (be careful; the brandy may ignite) and boil it for 30 seconds. Next, add the cream and boil it for 2 minutes. Transfer the sauce to a bowl and let it stand until it reaches room temperature. The sauce can be made up to 2 hours ahead.

Sprinkle the scallops with salt and pepper. Heat the vegetable oil in another large nonstick skillet over high heat and add the scallops. Turn the heat down to medium-high and cook until they are golden brown, about 2 minutes per side. Remove the scallops to a plate.

Add the juice to the same hot skillet. Boil it for 1 minute, scraping up the brown bits. Add the reserved sauce and bring it to a simmer. Remove the sauce from the heat.

Heat the remaining ½ tablespoon of olive oil in a large saucepan over medium-high heat. Add the garlic and stir for 30 seconds. Add the spinach; toss until it is barely wilted and still bright green, about 2 minutes. Season it with salt and pepper.

Using tongs, divide the spinach between eight plates, mounding it in the center. You can make this ahead of time and just keep it covered at room temperature. Arrange 1 scallop on each spinach mound. Spoon the brandy cream sauce over the scallops.

Note: Unfiltered fresh apple juice is thicker and has a more intense flavor than regular bottled apple juice. Look for it in the produce section on ice or in a refrigerator case.

FIG FLATBREAD WITH PARMESAN

SERVES 10 TO 12

12 slices white bread, crusts cut off
¼ cup (80 ml) fig jam
2 to 3 ounce (55 to 85 g) block of
   Parmigiano-Reggiano cheese

2 tablespoons extra-virgin olive oil
Fresh ground pepper

Preheat the oven to broil and position a rack 5 to 6 inches (12 to 15 cm) away from the broiler. Place the bread on a baking sheet and toast it for 2 minutes, flipping it halfway through, or until golden brown.

Spread 1 teaspoon of the jam on each piece of bread. Cut the bread in half diagonally. Using a vegetable peeler, make curls of Parmesan and place 2 or 3 on each bread triangle. Drizzle each with the oil and top with pepper.

10-Minute Happy Hour

This month, whip up a large batch of either the Sidecar (page 50) or the Mason Jar Basil Pisco Sour (page 51). If you opt for the vintage Sidecar, serve up some standard bar snacks such as the Simply Addictive Sugar and Spice Nuts (page 41). If you choose the lighter and tangier Pisco Sour, put out a plate of sliced or diced cantaloupe and honeydew wrapped in jamon or prosciutto along with small bowls of peanuts and almonds, and enjoy an easy happy hour in 10 minutes' time.

Pineapple Honey Bee, page 64

APRIL

chapter 4

VODKA

The Most Popular Pour at the Bar

Finally! For this month's cocktail club, you'll be toasting with the number one player in the cocktail game: vodka. Despite being snubbed by connoisseurs, the numbers don't lie—vodka beats every other spirit in bar sales, hands down.

It's not hard to see why this little pour is so popular. When you order vodka, there's no deciphering labels or vintages, and there is no wildly nuanced guessing game about how it will taste from brand to brand. It's virtually aroma free, pours crystal clear, is easy to drink, and plays nicely with all sorts of other ingredients in the shaker, typically taking on the flavor of whatever you mix it with.

Generally, you can tell vodkas apart by how "hot" they are, or how much they burn the back of your throat when you drink them. While vodka may not be laced with complex flavors or aromas, different brands can be distinguished by subtle personality differences like a sweet note or an oily mouthfeel. Purity—in the sense of lacking any real distinctions—is actually lauded in this spirit category. Tiny disparities are barely detectable when it's mixed up with juices, soda, or whatnot in a shaker, but tasting different vodkas straight up side by side might be eye opening if you've never had it pure before. This attribute gives vodka an open playing field, letting its cocktails venture into sweet, salty, bitter, and beyond.

The Vodka Situation

While vodka will prove to be the easiest spirit we'll navigate this year, there are just a couple of variations with which to familiarize yourself. First off, vodka is made all over the world, with the most renowned regions being Russia, Poland, and Sweden. America, Canada, France, the Netherlands, and the U.K. all make tons of it, too. The fact is, with the consumption rates so high, there is room for everyone to get in on this spirit successfully.

Here are some of the most widely recognized brands and their countries of origin:
- Russia: Stolichnaya (a.k.a. Stoli), Russian Standard, Popov
- Poland: Belvedere, Chopin
- Sweden: Absolut, Karlsson's, Level, Svedka
- America: SKYY, Hangar One, Charbay, Tito's Handmade
- France: Grey Goose, Pinnacle
- Canada: Crystal Head
- Finland: Finlandia
- Netherlands: Ketel One, Van Gogh, Vox
- United Kingdom: Smirnoff, Three Olives

Making Vodka

Vodka is what is called a "rectified" spirit. This means the spirit has undergone repeated distillation, and for most vodka that means it has been triple distilled. Vodka is then filtered, usually through charcoal, to remove any impurities, which are called *congeners* in the booze world. Crystal Head Vodka, packaged in a glass skull, is quadruple distilled, making it very smooth to drink. But they don't stop there—this vodka is

then filtered through 500-million-year-old crystals known as Herkimer diamonds. Lots of other brands belly up for this boozy throwdown and make all sorts of claims in order to distinguish themselves from other brands. One may use diamond dust, another rare sands, and a third might use quartz for filtering, with each claiming to produce a better-tasting vodka than the others ("better tasting" meaning "better feeling or smoother drinking," since most unflavored vodka has very little taste).

The Heart of It

Besides its birthplace, another difference that can impact flavor is a vodka's main ingredient. Vodka can be distilled from grains—such as wheat, barley, or rye, and even corn, as in the case of Tito's Handmade. It can also be produced from potatoes and sometimes it is made from distilled spirits of fruits or sugar. Among connoisseurs (I even chuckle writing that), vodka from rye and wheat are considered the finest.

Typically, it is virtually impossible to distinguish the main ingredient in the vodkas we drink today. Don't take my word for it: Taste test a chilled glass of Chopin—a potato vodka from Poland—against Absolut—a Swedish vodka made from wheat—and see if you can taste wheat or potatoes. Chances are you will not be able to distinguish the main ingredient.

Taste Test

A spirit's body, or the feel of the spirit in your mouth (a.k.a. mouthfeel), does tend to range slightly from brand to brand but, again, once mixed with other ingredients, even these slight differences are hard to recognize. For a mouthfeel face-off, pour a glass of chilled Absolut next to a chilled Stolichnaya and taste test. Notice the Absolut has a fuller mouthfeel, or body. It can be smooth, even oily, with a slightly sweet finish. The Stoli, made from wheat and rye, is lighter and clean on the palate, with a slightly herbal or medicinal quality and no sweet send-off, typical of Russian vodkas overall. If you're a big white wine drinker and you choose full-bodied Chardonnay over the lighter, cleaner mouthfeel of Sauvignon Blanc, you'll probably prefer Absolut when it's poured straight up.

Clear Vodka vs. Flavored Vodka

What's your favorite ice cream? I bet they have a vodka in that flavor! Flavors that originally seemed cutting edge like Absolut Citron, a must for your *Sex and the City*-inspired Cosmos of the 1990s, or a fancy schmancy Grey Goose l'Orange martini, are timid in comparison to today's flavor choices like birthday cake, s'mores, quince, saffron, root beer, bacon, or blueberry-pomegranate. The category continues to grow and it's not just names of fruits, candy, and other edibles you'll find in flavored vodka. You can now buy vodka *experiences* like "Loopy," "Dude," or even "Purple." With flavored vodkas, your happy hour options have become infinite.

PARTY FAVOR

No need to have your glassware live in your freezer! To get a frosty patina, just rinse your glass in cold water and chill it in the freezer for 30 minutes before your guests arrive. You can also fill your glass with ice water and let it chill while you are mixing the drink, tossing out the ice and wiping down the glass before use. Avoid the freezer for fine crystal, because this is more delicate and cracks easily if exposed to freezing temperatures.

Hangover Helpers

Since vodka is so easy to drink, it might not sink in that you've had one too many until it's too late. Everyone has their own ideas for how to cure a hangover, and around the globe there are different rituals to tame the beast. For instance, the vodka-loving Russians believe that drinking pickle juice helps. There is no cure-all for hangovers, but there are things that help. Here's the skinny on some popular myths and what you actually should be doing to curb a hangover and ease the pain.

- *Avoid greasy food.* While it may feel good going down after a night of cocktails, greasy food can actually make you feel worse. Instead make sure to eat *before* you drink.
- *Skip the coffee.* Caffeine can irritate an already uneasy stomach and exacerbate your dehydration.
- *Indulge in eggs.* They have an amino acid called cysteine that actually helps break down hangover-induced toxins.
- *Ginger root is the cure.* Again there is no cure-all, but ginger ale, ginger chews, or ginger candy will help soothe your stomach.
- *Grab a banana!* Bananas, and even kiwis, will help put lost electrolytes back in the body.
- *Make a hangover kit.* You never know when one after-work drink may turn into more, so keep a little hangover kit including breath freshener, ibuprofen, a bottle of water, and sunglasses in your car or at your desk.

PARTY FAVOR

The term "happy hour" originated back in the 1920s with the United States Navy, where the expression was used to indicate leisure time for the servicemen and -women. U.S. Navy cocktail club guidelines advise you all to preserve the tradition of celebrating that much-needed leisure time!

Different from happy hour, cocktail hour—typically the hour before dinner is served—began making an appearance during the Prohibition era. The daring types (a.k.a. fun friends) would venture into speakeasys, illegal underground establishments that served alcohol, and indulge for an hour before they headed out for a supper on the town. Whether you call yours happy hour or cocktail hour, or use both interchangeably, I'm sure you'll agree that they rarely last only an hour.

Get Your Drink On!

As we mentioned previously, vodka doesn't bring a whole lot to the glass in terms of flavor and aromas. So this month, what you'll be looking for in the different pours is more about mouthfeel. Pay attention to how smooth it goes down: Does it burn or does it feel creamy? Do you like the way it tastes once you've swallowed your sip? Once again, we have a great mix of vintage cocktails, like the Basic Bloody Mary (page 62), and new cocktails like the Pineapple Honey Bee (page 64), so let's get to sipping!

Tips for This Month

This month, you'll need a cleared-off counter space, side table, or bar cart to set up your Bloody Mary bar. If you plan on making the Pineapple Honey Bee cocktail, it's a good idea to get a pitcher and gather some mason jars ahead of time.

❦ The Classics ❧

BASIC BLOODY MARY

SERVES 1

Ice cubes
½ cup (120 ml) tomato juice
1½ teaspoons freshly squeezed lemon juice
1½ ounces vodka
4 dashes of hot sauce (traditionally
    Tobasco)

2 dashes of Worcestershire sauce
Pinch of celery salt
Pinch of fresh ground pepper
1 celery stalk, for garnish
1 lemon wedge, for garnish

Add all of the ingredients except for the garnishes to a mixing glass or shaker filled with ice. Stir to chill.

Strain the mixture into a pint glass half full with ice. Garnish with the celery stalk and lemon wedge.

BLOODY MARY BAR

A Bloody Mary bar is a must for brunch, but can be just as much fun for happy hour, too. It's also a great way to save on time, since small glasses filled with ice can be preset for guests to serve themselves. Encourage guests to use only 1 tablespoon (½ ounce) of vodka for each taster drink if they're having other cocktails to taste at cocktail club.

Here are some ideas for accoutrements you can add to your spread for a DIY drink bar sure to please everyone in your crew:

- **The Base:** Start off with your favorite tomato juice (you may offer Clamato, too) and set up ingredients for guests to build their own.
- **The Spirits:** Here you can offer a variety of flavored vodkas. Some of my favorites in Bloody Marys are citron, bacon, pepper, and jalapeño.
- **The Heat:** Include a sampling of canned chipotle peppers, wasabi paste, horseradish, jalapeño peppers, Old Bay seasoning, and a selection of hot sauces.
- **Garnish Galore:** A bamboo cocktail skewer filled with some of the Quick Spicy Pickled Vegetables on page 68 coupled with a fresh celery stalk is my favorite way to garnish a Bloody Mary. Also delicious are pickled brussels sprouts, baby white turnips, caper berries, pickled string beans, a choice of marinated olives, celery, beef jerky, pickled carrots, pickled radishes, cocktail onions, and lemon wedges.

Finally, put out a small plate of salt and pepper with extra lemon wedges for guests to rim their glasses.

HARVEY WALLBANGER

The sordid story of how this drink got its name has to do with a surfer who'd consume too much and end up bumping into the walls. Thus, the Harvey Wallbanger. Essentially this is a Screwdriver with the Italian herbal liqueur Galliano added.

1½ ounces vodka
½ cup (120 ml) orange juice
¼ ounce Galliano liqueur

In an ice-filled highball or tall glass, pour the vodka and orange juice in together, then float the Galliano on top.

SHAKE IT UP

Harvey's Mexican cousin is named Freddie Fudpucker. For this cocktail, substitute tequila for the vodka.

ᓚ New Twists ᓚ

PINEAPPLE HONEY BEE

SERVES 4 TO 6

This cocktail calls for a new flavored vodka: pineapple honey, from the Little Black Dress Vodka collection. Made ahead and served in mason jars, it's perfect for a party. This recipe is for a bigger batch, but it can easily be halved depending on how many are attending your cocktail club this month.

2 tablespoons honey
¼ cup (60 ml) warm water
1 cup (240 ml) pineapple or pineapple
   honey-flavored vodka
¼ cup (60 ml) freshly squeezed lemon juice,
   strained

½ cup loosely packed fresh basil leaves
Angostura bitters
Club soda
Lemon slices, for garnish

Dissolve the honey in the warm water. This can easily be done by combining the honey and water and warming it in a microwave for 30 seconds.

In a small pitcher, combine the vodka, honey water, and lemon juice. Add a couple of leaves of basil and 2 dashes of bitters to 4 to 6 mason jars or glasses and muddle with a wooden spoon.

When you're ready to serve, fill the mason jars or glasses with ice cubes and divide the cocktail evenly among the glasses. Top each with club soda. Garnish with the lemon slices and serve.

DIRTY MARTINI

In January's cocktail club, we established that a Martini was originally made with gin. However, ask most bartenders today what they reach for when someone orders a Martini and their answer will be vodka, a change that probably came about due to the rise in popularity of drinking dirty martinis. Olives love vodka and a bit of vermouth, so try it "dirty" this month and see if you do too.

Ice cubes
3 ounces (90 ml) vodka
1 dash of dry Vermouth

1½ teaspoons olive brine, or more
* depending how dirty you like it*
2 olives, for garnish

In a shaker filled with ice, combine the vodka, vermouth, and olive brine. Shake until well chilled. Strain the mixture into a chilled martini glass and garnish with the olives.

WHITE COSMO

SERVES 1

We all know about the traditional Cosmopolitan cocktail, but this one brings a gorgeous new bottle to your bar with the addition of the elderflower liqueur from St. Germain.

Ice cubes
¼ cup (60 ml) vodka
1 ounce St. Germain liqueur
1½ tablespoons white cranberry juice

1 tablespoon freshly squeezed lime or lemon
* juice*
Lime or lemon wedge or twist, for garnish

In a cocktail shaker filled with ice, add all of the ingredients except for the garnish. Shake until chilled. Strain the mixture into a chilled martini glass and garnish.

KIWI VODKA TONIC

SERVES 2

This recipe calls for kiwis, but almost any fruit or herb combination, such as blueberry and lavender, will work alongside the tonic in this simple cocktail.

1 kiwi, peeled
2 teaspoons plain or mint-infused simple
* syrup (page 15)*
Ice cubes

3 ounces (90 ml) vodka
Tonic water
2 lime wedges

Slice 2 wheels (or rounds) of kiwi and roughly chop the rest. Divide the chopped kiwi and simple syrup between two rocks glasses. Lightly muddle together the simple syrup and kiwi.

Fill the glasses three-quarters full with ice. Divide the vodka evenly between the two glasses. Top each with tonic and add a squeeze of lime to each glass. Stir. Garnish each glass with a kiwi wheel to finish.

❦ Eat Up! ❧

Your Bloody Mary bar goes rockstar with the addition of Quick Spicy Pickled Veggies (page 68) and a simple-to-prepare plate of smoked salmon and crème fraîche is perfect alongside a cold Kiwi Vodka Tonic. No need to be a trained chef to whip up some knock-out nibbles: Each of this month's dishes is simple to prepare, with impressive results that even a kitchen rookie can achieve.

SMOKED SALMON WITH CAPERS, CRÈME FRAICHE, AND PRESERVED LEMON

SERVES 12

24 good-quality water or seeded crackers
4 ounces (115 g) thinly sliced smoked
   salmon
4 ounces (120 ml) crème fraîche, store-
   bought or homemade (recipe follows)

3 tablespoons capers
2 to 3 tablespoons thinly slivered preserved
   lemon, or 2 tablespoons grated lemon
   zest

Top each of the crackers with an equal amount of the salmon. Dollop each with about 1½ teaspoons crème fraîche, sprinkle on a few capers, and finish with lemon slivers or a sprinkling of zest.

HOMEMADE CRÈME FRAÎCHE

MAKES ABOUT 2 CUPS (480ML)

2 cups (480 ml) heavy cream   2 tablespoons low-fat buttermilk

Gently heat the cream and buttermilk to between 85° (30°C) and 105°F (40°C) on a candy thermometer. This happens quickly, so do it on your stovetop on the lowest heat setting and don't walk away. Pour the mixture into a glass jar and allow it to thicken overnight at room temperature (68° to 72°F/20°C to 22°C). The next day, stir it and place it in the refrigerator for 1 more day of thickening. It will keep for up to 2 weeks, but probably won't last that long!

QUICK SPICY PICKLED VEGGIES

SERVES 12 TO 14

Serve these delicious pickled vegetables with some toothpicks for your guests to enjoy.

2 cups (480 ml) distilled white vinegar
  (5%)
¼ cup (75 g) pickling salt
2 teaspoons dill seed
1½ teaspoons cayenne pepper
8 ounces (225 g) fresh green beans,
  trimmed and cut into 1-inch (2.5-cm)
  pieces

6 jalapeño peppers, cut into ¼-inch (6-mm)
  rounds (seeded, for less heat)
3 medium carrots, peeled and cut in 1-inch
  (2.5-cm) sections on the bias
1½ cups (186 g) bite-size cauliflower florets
6 cloves garlic, peeled and slightly crushed

Add the vinegar, 2 cups (480 ml) of water, and salt to a saucepan and bring them to a boil over medium heat, stirring to dissolve the salt. Remove from the heat and add the dill seed and cayenne pepper.

In a clean quart jar or glass bowl, add vegetables to about ½ inch (12 mm) below the rim. Pour in the warm vinegar mixture to cover the vegetables.

Let them cool to room temperature. Put the lid on the jar or cover the bowl tightly with plastic wrap, and refrigerate the vegetables for at least 24 hours or up to 1 week.

Note: As an added bonus, there will be some brine left over, which you can store in the refrigerator and use to pickle something else.

TOMATOES, VODKA, AND SALT

SERVES 10 TO 12

24 cherry or grape tomatoes
Vodka

Coarse salt like kosher, sea, or fleur de sel

Pour a little vodka in the bottom of an olive tray (see Note) and place a single row of tomatoes right on top. Serve them with toothpicks and a side of coarse salt in a small bowl. Guests should prick a vodka-soaked cherry tomato and then just barely dip it into the small dish of salt to coat the bottom. This little hors d' oeuvre couldn't be easier to assemble or more fun to eat!

Note: You can find long, narrow olive trays or dishes at most home stores or specialty kitchen shops.

10-Minute Happy Hour

This month, our 10-minute happy hour couldn't be easier with a batch of Kiwi Vodka Tonics (page 66). Serve them alongside some pita with a store-bought spicy raita or tzatziki and you've got a spicy snack paired with the perfect complementary cool cocktail for a brilliant happy hour in no time.

White Peach Julep, page 79

MAY

chapter 5

WHISKEY

From the Scottish Highlands to Churchill Downs

This month is exploding with excuses to clink glasses. We're heading back to the dark side—or, should I say, brown side—of spirits this month with a foray into the world of whiskey. For any first-timers, whether it's called whiskey, bourbon, Tennessee, rye, Canadian, Japanese, Irish, or Scotch, it's all whiskey.

No matter where it's from, all whiskey is distilled from fermented grain mash and aged in oak, typically charred American white oak. The grain can be barley, malted barley, rye, malted rye, wheat, corn, or a combination of them. They can also vary in style, alcohol content, and, of course, quality.

Whiskey or Whisky? The spelling of this spirit varies, but often it's indicated by the booze's country of origin. The Scottish drop the "e," as do the Japanese and Canadians. The Irish and Americans spell it with the "e." Like most spirits, whiskey is made all over the world, but a simple trick to remember how to spell the most popular ones is that countries with an "e" in their names like the United States and Ireland spell it with an "e" and the plural is whiskeys. Countries with no "e" in their names, like Scotland, Japan, and Canada, spell it whisky (no "e") and the plural is whiskies. There are exceptions to every rule, of course, so don't be dismayed if you see an American whiskey spelled without the "e."

The Key Players

Irish Whiskey Irish whiskey tends to be sweeter than Scotch, yet not as sweet as some bourbons. It's smooth and easy to sip. On the Emerald Isle, they are mixing it with all sorts of ingredients for fun cocktails, but straight up or on the rocks with ginger ale is my preferred way to go. A couple of brands to seek out are Jameson and Kilbeggan.

Scotch Whisky For some reason, Scotch is the one spirit most cocktail newbies consistently skip—in fact, they fear it. It's definitely an acquired taste, but don't skip the Scotch just because it isn't love at first sip. This one needs a little time to make its way into your heart.

Scotch is made the same way other whiskeys are, but there is a unique element incorporated when drying the malt. They burn peat, a funky-smelling organic matter that imparts a very particular taste and aroma into the booze. Peat is such a unique element that you really have to experience it first-hand. Once you do, it will indelibly be imprinted on your brain. From then on, when you stick your nose into a glass of peaty Scotch whisky, you will certainly know it! When a Scotch is peaty, you will be able to detect more woodsy (campfire, burning earth) aromas, and sometimes even Band-Aid, not just the sweeter, smoky tobacco or bacon characteristics you may find in other spirits.

Taste Test

This month, pour a sip of Jameson Irish Whiskey next to a Scotch whisky from Islay. This is the fastest way to understand what peat lends to whiskey. Your Irish whiskey will be sweeter in aroma and taste, while the Islay Scotch whisky will blow you away with the strong aroma of smoke, burnt rubber, and even Band-Aid. Now you know what peaty means, and I'm sure you won't soon forget it.

In the case of Johnnie Walker, the world's best-selling Scotch whisky, you are sipping a blend that comes from all over Scotland. For the single malts, there are 4 main regions of production:

- **Islay and the Islands:** These heavily peated pours are hard to find a spot for in the shaker. Stick to sipping them solo, as their bold personalities don't play very nicely with other flavors. Famous distilleries here are Ardbeg, Laphroig, Lagavulin, and, my personal favorite, Bowmore.
- **Highlands:** This is the biggest of the areas, home to the famous Talisker, Dewar's, Oban, and Glenmorangie, to name a few distilleries. These Scotches are typically dry, smooth, and smoky.
- **Lowlands:** This area produces milder whisky than that of the Highlands. Distilleries here are Glenkinchie, Bladnoch, and Auchentoshan.

- **Speyside**: Cleverly named for its placement beside the River Spey, whiskys from the Speyside region have a light, sweet character. Names you may recognize are Glenfiddich, Aberlour, Glenlivet, and Macallan.

American Whiskey There are two main categories of whiskey in America: straight or blended. Straight whiskey includes bourbon, Tennessee, and rye. Lucky for us, all of these love a go at the shaker, providing us with a wide variety of delicious cocktails.

- **Bourbon**: Born in Kentucky over 200 years ago, this whiskey, made mostly of a corn mash, is known for being sweet and smooth. Bourbon grains are rich in sugar, fruit, and spice, which you can easily taste in a pour. Earthiness and smokiness come from the oak barrels used for aging. While lots of delicious bourbon pours from Kentucky, it is a common misconception that it can only be made there. Bourbon can be produced in any of the fifty states and, in fact, the rise in popularity of small-batch bourbon can be seen all over the country.
- **Rye Whiskey**: This is made from a grain mixture that's mostly rye, and the rest can be corn, wheat, malted rye, malted barley, or a combination of any of the above. Then, like bourbon, it's aged in new toasted oak barrels. The resulting flavors are similar to bourbon but tend to be more robust and spicy and often finish on the bitter side.
- **Tennessee Whiskey**: Tennessee is probably the most popular of the American whiskeys, with the Jack Daniel's Distillery hosting up to 250,000 visitors every year. It's Disneyland for adults! Tennessee whiskey is made just like bourbon, but is produced only in the state of Tennessee and it undergoes filtering through maple charcoal, which is also called Lincoln County Process. Other producers here are George Dickel and Benjamin Prichard's.

SPEAKEASY

All bourbon is made using the sour mash method, which means that a bit of the mash used in the previous batch of bourbon is held over and added to the fresh mash. The old mash, a.k.a. setback, is sour (hence the name) and creates a great environment for yeast to grow and thus ferment the mash.

All booze begins with water, so a high-quality water source is ideal when whipping up spirits. Kentucky has large limestone reservoirs, which produce water that's relatively soft and free from iron and other contaminants, making it an ideal ingredient for their bourbon.

The Types

Whiskey makers all have their own take on this spirit. The guide below will help you decipher labels when you're out shopping.

Blended Whiskey is made of both malt and grain whiskey, and its age is determined by the youngest whiskey in the blend. It is often made with other neutral spirits and sometimes even caramel coloring and flavoring.

Single Malts are made from one particular grain in a single distillery.

Blended Malt Whiskey is a mixture of single malt whiskeys from different distilleries.

Cask Strength, Barrel Proof, or Over-proof whiskeys are uncut and bottled straight from the cask, giving them a higher proof. This exposes the secret of the trade, which is that most distilled spirits are diluted with water before bottling to make them more palatable.

Single Cask or Single Barrel whiskeys come from one cask. You will usually find a bottle and barrel number on the label.

What is White Whiskey? All whiskey comes off the still clear; it's the aging in the oak barrels that gives it the gorgeous auburn to caramel colors and its nutty and vanilla flavors. White whiskey, also known as raw whiskey or "new make," is sometimes referred to as *moonshine* or *white dogs*. This version is stripped down and has a very pungent smell. In this form, you can tell what the different base grains offer on their own without the flavors oak barrels impart. These days, white whiskeys are a far cry from their moonshine days. Much more palatable than the white dogs of the past, sweet aged white whiskeys are popping up all over the place, possibly to compete in the cocktail craze with the likes of vodka, gin, rum, and tequila. Small-batch distillers love it because they can sell something immediately without waiting for all of their product to mature, and adventurous palates are always tracking down the latest trend to taste.

Small-Batch Bourbon The DIY craze alongside the bourbon boom has led to a spike in small-batch bourbon production. Small-batch means limited quantity (higher-priced) handcrafted bourbon from individual recipes that provide all sorts of unique tasting experiences. Typically, these small-batch bourbons pour up a pre-Prohibition style of booze, meaning they are in your face with flavor and aromas and often are higher proof.

How To Make Cracked Ice Cracked ice is typically the ice of choice for cocktails because it cools drinks more quickly than extra-large cubes (you often see them used at high-end cocktail bars) and doesn't melt as fast as shaved or crushed ice does. The way to achieve cracked ice for a single cocktail is to wrap the cubes in a clean tea towel and whack them with the outside of a spoon a couple of times until they break apart. The crushed ice setting on most refrigerator/freezer units is not the same as cracked ice. If you need cracked ice for a crowd, simply fill a gallon-size zip-top bag about half full with regular ice cubes. Seal it and use a kitchen mallet or rolling pin to crack the cubes.

❦ Get Your Drink On! ❧

Whiskey cocktails can be spicy or sweet, and range from super strong to better balanced. Here are some descriptors you might find helpful as you make your way around a glass of whiskey or bourbon: nutty, vanilla, fruity, orange, caramel, smoky, sweet, molasses, leather, tobacco, earthy, apricot, floral, spicy, woody, toffee, and honey. We'll get a good mix of each with our cocktail picks this month: We'll take the classic Old-Fashioned and turn it orange, stir up a Manhattan, and taste test a Sazerac. The traditional Mint Julep gets an infusion of white peaches and we'll stick to Southern roots with the Good Doctor, a Dr Pepper and bourbon drink. Last, but not least, we'll try the Kentucky Corpse Reviver, basically a version of delicious bourbon-loaded lemonade.

Tips for This Month
It's All in the Glass
This month, we cover the gamut on glassware. Our line-up calls for almost all the players, including martini, old-fashioned, coupe or wine glasses, and highballs, too. If you are going to be sipping whiskey straight up, connoisseurs like a small tulip-shaped glass. This is preferred because the aromas concentrate in the neck of the glass, letting you get a nice big whiff of it.

The Classics

MOM'S MANHATTAN

SERVES 1

It's only fitting that we include the Manhattan this month, as Mother's Day is upon us and this is my mother's signature cocktail. It's a ritual for her—stirred, rocks on the side, with one cherry nestled in the soft "V" of a chilled martini glass. The rocks are added as you sip to keep your cocktail cool and have it last just a bit longer. The classic recipe calls for a couple of dashes of bitters, but this one is Mom's signature take, sans the bitters.

Ice cubes
¼ cup (60 ml) whiskey (My mom's choice is Canadian Club)

1 ounce sweet vermouth
Maraschino cherry, for garnish

In a cocktail shaker filled with ice, add the whiskey and vermouth. Stir until well chilled.

Strain the mix into a chilled martini glass and garnish with the cherry. Serve with ice on the side.

ORANGE OLD-FASHIONED

SERVES 1

This drink is so revered it even has a glass of its own. An old-fashioned glass is typically short—squat even—and this particular cocktail should be served in its particular glass. Here, we turn the classic old-fashioned orange by swapping the traditional Angostura bitters for an orange variety and garnishing with a fat orange peel.

1 sugar cube, or ½ teaspoon sugar
3 dashes of orange bitters (see Note)
Club soda

Large orange peel, for garnish
Ice cubes
¼ cup (60 ml) rye whiskey

Put the sugar in an old-fashioned or short rocks glass and add in the bitters and a splash of soda.

Use a muddler or a spoon to crush up the sugar until it dissolves. I like to add the orange peel here, too. Squeeze it to express the oils, run it around the rim of the glass, and muddle it right in with the bitters and sugar. This way you get an amazing fresh orange flavor into the cocktail.

Add in the ice and rye. Stir and enjoy.

Note: If you don't like orange, this sip is delicious with Angostura or root beer bitters, too. Just skip the peel.

SAZERAC

The Sazerac is the official drink of New Orleans. It's a classic cocktail similar to the Old-Fashioned, but it's amped up with rye instead of bourbon and gets an absinthe rinse. This cocktail calls for Peychaud's bitters, another New Orleans bar staple, but Angostura would do in a pinch.

> Absinthe
> 1 sugar cube, ½ teaspoon sugar, or 1½
>   teaspoons simple syrup (page 15)
> 4 to 5 dashes of Peychaud's bitters

> Ice cubes
> ¼ cup (60 ml) rye whiskey
> Lemon peel, for garnish

Rinse an old-fashioned or short rocks glass with absinthe (pour absinthe in and swirl it around to really coat the glass, then pour it out).

Add the sugar and bitters to the glass and muddle them together.

Add the ice and rye and stir. Garnish with the lemon peel and enjoy.

❦ New Twists ❧

KENTUCKY CORPSE REVIVER

Corpse Revivers are a category of drinks meant to act as "hair of the dog," or the alcohol you drink the day after a night of imbibing in hopes of curbing a hangover. This is a variation on the popular Corpse Reviver #2 (page 156), which uses gin.

> Ice cubes
> 1½ tablespoons bourbon
> 1½ tablespoons Cointreau

> 1½ tablespoons freshly squeezed lemon juice
> 1½ tablespoons Lillet Blanc
> Thinly sliced lemon, for garnish

Fill a cocktail shaker with ice. Add the bourbon, Cointreau, lemon juice, and Lillet Blanc.

Shake until your cocktail shaker forms a nice frost on the exterior.

Strain the mixture into a chilled coupe or wine glass. Top with the lemon and enjoy.

WHITE PEACH JULEP

SERVES 1

All right race fans, this version of the mint julep is awesome served on Derby day and is just peachy all summer long. If you can't find white peaches, feel free to use cling. Either way, be sure your peaches are fresh and ripe.

½ fresh white peach, pitted and diced,
   skin on
6 fresh mint leaves
¼ cup (60 ml) bourbon
1 ounce peach-flavored liqueur like Bols
   (you can substitute peach schnapps, but
   your sip will be a little sweeter)
2 dashes of bitters, peach if you can find it
Ice cubes
Club soda
White peach slice and mint sprig,
   for garnish

In a Collins glass, lightly muddle the diced peach with the mint leaves.

Add the bourbon, liqueur, bitters, and enough ice to fill the glass.

Top with a splash of club soda and lightly stir. Garnish with a peach slice and a sprig of mint.

THE GOOD DOCTOR

SERVES 1

This simple cocktail incorporates Amaro, a bittersweet Italian liqueur, with rye whiskey and the pep of Dr Pepper. Lots of whiskey drinks can be very serious, but this one is fun and leans to the sweeter side.

Ice cubes
1½ ounces Amaro Nonino (this one is
   sweeter), or any Amaro you prefer

1½ ounces rye whiskey
¾ cup (180 ml) Dr Pepper
Orange slice, for garnish

In a tall glass filled with ice, combine the Amaro and rye and top with the Dr Pepper.

Squeeze the orange and drop the slice into the glass.

℃ Eat Up! ℈

Whiskey lends itself to so many mouthwatering dishes—both as an ingredient and a great pairing on the side. It sings in savory cream sauces or sweet caramel sauces, and its smokiness enhances anything with bacon or barbecue sauce. In honor of bourbon's Southern roots, this month our snacks include a to-die-for Bacon-Whiskey Jam and Pimento Cheese Crostini (page 82) that is killer when paired with a Manhattan or Old-Fashioned. The Caramelized Onion Mac-n-Cheese Bites below work with just about every cocktail on our list this month, and the Edamame with Smoked Sea Salt (page 82) matches nicely with any smoky whiskey.

CARAMELIZED ONION MAC-N-CHEESE BITES

SERVES 12

2 tablespoons olive oil
1 medium onion, chopped (about 1½ cups/225 g)
Salt
Cooking spray
1 ounce (28 g) grated Parmesan cheese
8 ounces (225 g) elbow macaroni

2 tablespoons unsalted butter
2 tablespoons all-purpose flour
1 cup (240 ml) milk
4 ounces (115 g) grated cheddar cheese
4 ounces (115 g) grated Asiago cheese
1 large egg
Pinch of cayenne pepper

Heat the oil in a medium sauté pan over medium heat. Add the onion and a pinch of salt and cook until caramelized, about 12 to 15 minutes, adding a splash of water if the onions get dry.

Prepare a mini-muffin tin by spraying it with cooking spray and sprinkling in a bit of grated Parmesan to evenly coat the bottom of each cup. Set aside the rest of the cheese.

Meanwhile, cook the pasta until al dente according to package instructions, about 8 to 10 minutes. Drain and set aside.

Preheat the oven to 400°F/205°C.

In a medium saucepan, melt the butter and whisk in the flour until smooth. Cook for 2 minutes. Slowly whisk in the milk and cook until boiling, about 5 minutes. Slowly whisk in the grated cheeses, including the leftover Parmesan, and whisk until smooth and melted.

Remove the cheese mixture from the heat and stir in the egg and cayenne. Fold in the caramelized onions and cooked pasta. Spoon the mixture into the prepared mini muffin tins and bake for 10 minutes, or until brown and bubbly.

Allow the bites to cool for 10 minutes in the pan, then remove and cool another 5 minutes before serving. Serve them warm or at room temperature.

EDAMAME WITH SMOKED SEA SALT

SERVES 10 TO 12

1 (12- to 16-ounce/340- to 455-g) bag
frozen edamame in the pod

1 to 2 tablespoons smoked sea salt

Cook the edamame according to the package instructions. (I cook mine in a covered dish with ¼ cup/60 ml water in the microwave for 4 minutes.) Sprinkle them with the salt and serve immediately.

Note: If you can't find smoked sea salt, you can combine 1 tablespoon kosher or sea salt and ¼ teaspoon smoked paprika to sprinkle over the edamame.

BACON-WHISKEY JAM
AND PIMENTO CHEESE CROSTINI

SERVES 10 TO 12

Pimento cheese is a staple when it comes to comfort foods in the South. It can be served on white bread without the crust as a dainty tea sandwich or on a greasy breakfast egg sandwich. Here, I pair it with bacon for an appetizer you won't be able to resist.

For the bacon jam:
1 pound (455 g) bacon, cut into ½-inch
(12-mm) pieces
1 medium onion, finely diced (about 1
cup/100 g)
2 cloves garlic, minced
½ cup (120 ml) brewed coffee
⅓ cup (65 g) packed dark
brown sugar
⅓ cup (75 ml) maple syrup
¼ cup (60 ml) Jameson whiskey
¼ cup (60 ml) apple
cider vinegar
¼ cup (25 g) minced fresh jalapeño, seeded
Salt and fresh ground pepper

For the pimento cheese:
4 ounces (115 g) yellow cheddar cheese,
grated (see Note)
3 tablespoons mayonnaise
1½ tablespoons diced pimentos or roasted
red bell peppers
1 tablespoon grated yellow onion
Salt

½ slender baguette, sliced on the bias into 18 (¼- to ½-inch/6- to 12-mm) slices

Make the jam: Cook the bacon in a large sauté pan set over medium-high heat, until the fat is cooked out and the bacon is beginning to brown, about 12 to 14 minutes. Remove the bacon from the pan.

Pour off all but 1 tablespoon of the fat, reduce the heat to medium, and add the onion and garlic to the pan. Cook until they are soft and translucent, about 6 to 8 minutes.

Add the coffee, sugar, syrup, whiskey, vinegar, and jalapeño to the pan. Bring them to a boil and cook for 2 to 3 minutes more.

Add the bacon back to the pan and stir to combine. Simmer it slowly over low heat with the lid off for about 45 minutes, or until the liquid has a syrupy consistency. Taste and add salt and pepper if necessary. Remove it from the heat and let it cool.

Store the jam in an airtight container in the refrigerator for up to 1 week. Warm it to room temperature or slightly reheat it before serving.

Make the pimento cheese: In the bowl of a food processor, combine the cheese, mayonnaise, pimentos, onion, and a pinch of salt and purée until they are combined. Cover and refrigerate until ready to serve.

To assemble: Spread about 2 teaspoons of pimento cheese on each slice of bread, then top with ½ to 1 teaspoon of bacon jam. Serve immediately.

Note: It is important to use freshly grated cheese, as using any bagged preshredded cheese will affect the consistency, leaving you with a more curdled looking end product.

10-Minute Happy Hour

For this month's 10-minute happy hour, we're putting a twist on a tried and true food and drink combo. It's a given that beer goes great with pizza, but so does the Good Doctor (page 79)! This is like an adult soda—Dr Pepper with an Italian Amaro and a splash of spicy rye makes a simple cocktail that goes great with a hot cheesy slice. Typically this cocktail is garnished with an orange wheel, but when pairing with pizza I prefer it sans l'orange.

Basil-Wrapped Chili-Lime Mangoes
and The Pink Paloma, pages 94 and 89

JUNE

chapter 6

TEQUILA

From Shots to Sophistication

Summer is here, and for cocktail club that means it's tequila time! This year, we've already tasted clear spirits like vodka and gin and ventured to the dark side with brandy and whiskey. Tequila, a category all its own, falls somewhere in between, with varieties that range from clear and glossy to rich and amber in color. As you can imagine, just as with wine, the color of this pour will tip you off to how it was made and what sort of flavors you'll taste. From *blanco* to *añejo* all the way to *mezcal*, you'll be well equipped to shop, sip, and serve this spirit by the end of this month's cocktail club. So turn on some music, make some more ice, and let's get to tequila.

What is Tequila?
Made from the blue agave plant, tequila—according to Mexican law—can only be made in the province of Jalisco and the few surrounding areas of Guanajuato, Michoacan, Nayarit, and Tamaulipas. Just as a Chardonnay from a cold region will be different from a Chardonnay from a hot growing climate, tequila's taste changes according to the place where the blue agave grows, a quality known as "terroir." *Terroir* is a French term, used

to describe the region in which grapes are grown for wine. It includes elements that affect agriculture such as the soil and the weather. For tequila grown in the highlands north of the city of Tequila, the agave plants are much larger and produce sweeter nectar. The lowlands produce slightly smaller agave, and their juice is more herbaceous and earthy in flavor and aroma.

Shop Savvy Tequila comes in two main categories: *mixto* or 100% blue agave. A mixto is a mix of agave juice and other fermented sugars and unless a label states that the tequila is made from "100% blue agave," then it's a mixto. Often these tequilas are shipped in bulk and bottled elsewhere (sometimes even the U.S.), and they deliver a flavor that's less interesting and delicious than the real deal 100% blue agave tequilas.

The Piña The *piña* is the heart of tequila. *Piña* comes from the Spanish word for pineapple, but as far as tequila is concerned, the piña we're interested in is the succulent center of the agave plant, named for its large, pineapple-like appearance. The agave's piñas take anywhere from six to twelve years to mature. After they are harvested, they are roasted, steamed, or slowly baked to turn their starches into fermentable sugar. Then they get shredded into pulp and the agave juice is fully extracted. The pulp is discarded and the juice goes into its fermentation vats, either barrels or stainless steel tanks, then on to distillation, next the bottling, and finally into your mouth.

Is More Always Better? After the tequila ferments, or turns into alcohol, it is then distilled. By law, all tequila must pass through the distillation process twice. Some brands put the tequila through a third distillation. That makes the product softer and easier to drink, but many tequila connoisseurs believe this actually strips away the personality of the drink.

Silver, Gold & All the Other Types of Tequila

White, Blanco, Plato, or Silver This is aged for a maximum of thirty days in oak barrels or stainless-steel vats, and usually costs less than tequila labeled "gold." This kind of tequila has lovingly been called "firewater," and this pour is definitely hot on the palate—probably not the style you want to sip straight up, though its low price makes it the top choice for cocktails. In fact, anytime you've ever ordered a margarita—unless you've specified otherwise—you've been drinking this style of tequila.

Reposado means "rested," and this style of tequila takes a nap between two and twelve months in oak barrels, which gives it a gold tinge. These tend to be softer and easier to drink on their own than the silvers.

Gold, Jóven This is usually a blend of white tequila and *reposado*. It's aged for a minimum of one year, but no more than three years, in American oak barrels that formerly held whiskey. José Cuervo skips silver and starts their bottling line-up with their gold standard, Cuervo Gold, which also happens to be the best-known brand of tequila in the world.

Aged/Añejo These tequilas are aged over a year in oak barrels and are a gorgeous dark amber to maple color. These are richer and fuller-bodied sipping tequilas, not meant for cocktails. Since I mentioned "rich," you should know these sips don't come cheap.

Extra-Añejo These tequilas are aged a minimum of three years. Like the añejo, these are for sipping, not mixing.

Mezcal: Tequila's Bad-Boy Brother

When we talk tequila, we can't ignore mezcal. While each of these spirits comes from the agave plant, mezcal can come from a variety of agave, mainly the *Espadín* variety, whereas tequila can only be made from blue agave. The tequila industry is regulated but the mezcal business is not, so you never really know what you're getting in a bottle of mezcal.

Most mezcal comes from Oaxaca, Mexico. While tequila is required to be distilled twice, mezcal is only distilled once, meaning the spirit is usually a bit more bracing and not as refined. When making mezcal, the piñas are always roasted underground in rock pits and covered with dirt. The wood fires over which they are roasted lend the piñas all sorts of smoky, earthy, gritty qualities. Like tequila, mezcal also has a series of styles including the blanco, reposado, añejo, and pechuga.

What About the Worm?

It has often been mistakenly believed that tequila used to be bottled with a worm; however, it was actually mezcal that housed the little critter and, in fact, you can still find bottles of mezcal with a worm. As the legend goes, it is supposed to ward of evil spirits. Over the years, I have found the true purpose is to smoke out the least intelligent of your friends, as this will inevitably be the one who offers to eat it.

Taste Test

If you're curious about mezcal, set up a blind taste test for this month's cocktail club. Choose one tequila and one mezcal to taste side by side. Remember: This is a tasting, not a shot contest. So swirl, sniff, and just lightly sip to experience the differences these two spirits offer.

❧ Get Your Drink On! ❧

Now we're getting to the best part—the drinks! Tequila can lend all sorts of aromas to cocktails this month, ranging from smoky to herbal and spicy. Tequila tastes can range from briny to floral, and even sweet. Most of the cocktails call for the more neutral silver tequila, but you may substitute gold if you wish. Using silver tequila will give your drinks a lighter body with a shorter finish, whereas using gold or aged tequila will lend your drinks a richer mouthfeel and longer finish. Either way it's time to grab your shakers and get to sipping!

Tips for This Month

It's All in the Glass Margarita glasses are fun for flair, but not necessary for this month. If you've got them, use them, but you can serve all of this month's drinks in highball glasses, double old-fashioned glasses, or even all-purpose wine glasses.

❧ The Classics ☙

THE FAMOUS MARGARITA

SERVES 1

The Margarita is by far the most popular tequila cocktail at the bar. This month, we'll make the classic Margarita cocktail from scratch to experience a lively, vibrant sip unlike today's sugar and preservative-laden mixes available by the bucket.

Ice cubes
1½ ounces silver tequila
1½ ounces Cointreau

1½ ounces freshly squeezed lime juice
Lime wedges
Coarse salt, for rimming the glasses

In a cocktail shaker filled with ice, combine the tequila, Cointreau, and lime juice and shake until nice and cold.

Run the lime wedge along the rim of the glass and dip the moistened rim into the salt. Fill the glass with ice and strain in the shaker's contents.

SHAKE IT UP

Most empty calories come from mixers, sodas, syrups, and sugared rims. For a low-calorie option, skip all the spirit accessories and sip tequila on the rocks with a wedge of lime and a spritz of club soda instead. This is a super slimmed down version of the margarita, and a refreshing cocktail perfectly suited for the summer months.

THE PINK PALOMA

SERVES 1

The Paloma is a drink as beloved, if not more so, than the Margarita, depending upon which bar you belly up to. The Paloma is a traditional Mexican cocktail made with grapefruit soda called Jarritos and, of course, tequila. My version recreates those flavors with freshly squeezed pink grapefruit juice and a touch of Perrier Pink Grapefruit for the spritz. If you can't find the pink grapefruit–flavored Perrier, you can use plain club soda instead.

¼ cup (60 ml) silver tequila
⅓ cup (75 ml) freshly squeezed pink
  grapefruit juice (about half a 4-inch/10-
  cm grapefruit)
Ice cubes

Sugar or simple syrup (page 15, optional)
2 lime wedges
Coarse salt (optional)
3 ounces (90 ml) Perrier Pink Grapefruit or
  club soda

The Pink Paloma, page 89

Add the tequila and the grapefruit juice to a cocktail shaker filled with ice. You can also add sugar or simple syrup if your grapefruits are not sweet enough on their own. Shake until chilled.

If you like a salted rim, run a lime wedge around the edge of the glass and dip the rim into a shallow plate with salt. Strain the drink into the glass. Top it with Perrier and serve with an additional lime wedge for garnish.

❦ New Twists ❧

STRAWBERRY-BASIL MARGARITAS

SERVES 8 TO 10

Margaritas have morphed over the years from simple citrus, lightly sweetened tequila cocktails into basically any tequila-based drink, either blended or on the rocks. Whether you go for the classic lime or this modern version, it's the perfect beverage for warm weather.

1 cup (200 g) sugar
Zest of 1 lime
10 to 12 strawberries, hulled and sliced
8 fresh basil leaves

2 to 2½ cups (480 to 600 ml) silver tequila
1 to 1½ cups freshly squeezed lime juice, strained
Ice cubes

In a small saucepan, combine the sugar and zest with 1 cup (240 ml) of water. Simmer over medium-high heat until the sugar is dissolved and strain the syrup into a clean container. Let it cool completely.

Add the strawberries to a large pitcher. Bruise or gently squeeze the basil leaves and add them to the pitcher. Add the tequila, lime-flavored simple syrup, and 1 cup of the lime juice and stir. Taste and adjust with more lime juice if desired. Cover and refrigerate overnight.

Serve in tall glasses filled with ice.

YELLOW JACKET COCKTAIL

SERVES 1

Ice cubes
¼ cup (60 ml) Cuervo Gold tequila
1 ounce yellow Chartreuse liqueur

1 dash of lemon bitters
1 tablespoon honey
1 lemon twist

In a cocktail glass filled with ice, add the tequila, Chartreuse, and bitters and stir to combine.

Microwave the honey for 15 to 30 seconds and drizzle the loosened honey on top. Add the lemon twist and serve the drink with a swizzle stick or stirrer.

Ginger Blackberry Smash,
opposite

GINGER-BLACKBERRY SMASH

SERVES 1

1 cup (200g) sugar
One 4-inch (10-cm) piece fresh ginger,
   peeled and sliced
2 teaspoons coarse salt
1 teaspoon ground ginger
1 lime wedge

Ice cubes
¼ cup (60 ml) silver tequila
1 ounce freshly squeezed lime juice
3 fresh blackberries
1 thin slice crystallized ginger

In a small saucepan, combine the sugar and fresh ginger with 1 cup (240 ml) of water. Bring them to a simmer over medium-high heat and stir until all of the sugar is dissolved. Let the ginger steep over low heat for about 20 minutes, or longer if you want your cocktail spicier. Then strain the syrup into a clean container and let it cool completely.

On a shallow plate, combine the salt and ground ginger. Use the lime wedge to moisten the rim of a glass and dip it lightly into the ginger and salt mixture.

In a shaker filled with ice, add the tequila, 1 ounce of the ginger-flavored simple syrup, and the lime juice, and shake until chilled.

Lightly muddle the blackberries in the bottom of your glass, then add ice. Strain the shaker into the glass and garnish it with a sliver of crystallized ginger.

HOMEMADE SUN TEA WITH TEQUILA

SERVES 8 TO 10

Pitcher drinks are perfect for outdoor parties and picnics. Premixed batches of adult iced tea keep you from having to play bartender and let everyone enjoy summer with a little swerve.

2 quarts (2 L) warm water
1 lemon, sliced
1 orange, sliced
4 black tea bags

1 cup (240 ml) simple syrup (page 15) or
   agave syrup
2 cups (480 ml) silver tequila
Ice cubes
Fresh mint sprigs, for garnish

In a large pitcher, add the water, sliced lemon and orange, and tea bags. Be sure to keep the paper tags on the tea hanging on the outside of the pitcher. Cover and place the pitcher in direct sunlight for 3 to 4 hours.

Once the tea is done steeping, add the simple syrup and tequila. Pour the tea into ice-filled mason jars or glasses and add a sprig of mint for garnish.

❦ Eat Up! ❧

I don't know about you, but I've worked up an appetite with all this tequila talk, which is perfect timing because our grub line-up this month is stellar. Pair the Basil-Wrapped Chili-Lime Mangoes below with a refreshing margarita or fire up your grill for some lip smacking Grilled Lamb Chops with Tequila–Brown Sugar Glaze (page 97) and a Yellow Jacket Cocktail (page 91) beside it. You can't go wrong with Deviled Eggs Three Ways (page 96)—especially if you're sipping a Ginger-Blackberry Smash (page 93) too!

BASIL-WRAPPED CHILI-LIME MANGOES

SERVES 10 TO 12

1 ripe mango, peeled and cut into 20 to 24 fingers
Juice of 1 lime

½ teaspoon chili powder
20 to 24 large fresh basil leaves

Toss the mango slices with the lime juice. Evenly sprinkle them with the chili powder and wrap 1 basil leaf around each piece, securing it with a toothpick.

EDIBLE WATERMELON MARGARITAS

SERVES 12

Some margaritas are served on the rocks, some are frozen, and some you can eat!

Ice cubes
1½ ounces silver tequila
1 tablespoon Cointreau
1 tablespoon freshly squeezed lime juice

12 (1-inch/2.5-cm) wedges fresh watermelon
Coarse salt, for garnish

Fan the sliced watermelon on a rimmed plate. The plate or platter needs a slightly raised rim so the cocktail does not pour out. Place the plate in the freezer for about 20 minutes to get an icy chill on your melon without freezing it solid.

In an ice-filled shaker, combine the tequila, Cointreau, and lime juice.

Strain the cocktail over the watermelon. I recommend putting your plate or platter where you will be serving it and then pour the drink over the watermelon slices to avoid spilling during transit.

Serve the coarse salt in a small bowl alongside for guests to sprinkle on their edible margarita.

DEVILED EGGS THREE WAYS

SERVES 10 TO 12

1 dozen large eggs
½ cup (120 ml) mayonnaise

1 teaspoon white or apple cider vinegar

For the chipotle:

1 teaspoon chopped chipotle pepper from a
can

1 teaspoon adobo sauce (from chipotles)
Pinch of salt

For the double dill:

1 tablespoon dill pickle relish
1 tablespoon chopped fresh dill, plus a bit
for garnish

Pinch of salt

For the salami and black olive:

2 tablespoons small-dice salami

1 tablespoon chopped black olives,
plus some slices for garnish

Put all the eggs in a large pot and cover them with about 1 inch (2.5 cm) of water. Set the pot over high heat and bring it to a full boil. Once the eggs are at a full boil, remove the pot from the heat, place the lid on, and allow the eggs to sit in the hot water for 10 minutes.

Drain the water off the eggs and run them under cold water. Peel the eggs and cut each one in half lengthwise. Remove the yolks and place them in a small bowl. Refrigerate the whites.

Combine the yolks, mayonnaise, and vinegar and whisk until they are smooth and creamy. (This yields about 1¼ cups/280 g.) Divide the yolk mixture into three small bowls, about ⅓ cup plus 1 tablespoon (90 ml/85 g) each. Add the chipotle, adobo sauce, and salt to one bowl; the relish, dill, and salt to another; and the salami and olives to the third bowl.

Put each of the mixtures in a quart-size zip-top bag. Cut a corner off each bag and use it like a pastry bag to fill the reserved whites evenly. Top each of the dill-filled eggs with a small sprig of fresh dill and the salami and black olive eggs with a sliced olive. Cover loosely and refrigerate until ready to serve.

GRILLED LAMB CHOPS
WITH TEQUILA–BROWN SUGAR GLAZE

SERVES 8, WITH EXTRA GLAZE

For the glaze:

1 cup (240 ml) gold or añejo tequila

¼ cup (50 g) packed dark brown sugar

2 tablespoons adobo sauce (from chipotles)

1 whole chipotle pepper from a can, seeded and minced

For the lamb:

1 rack of lamb with 8 bones

1 tablespoon olive oil

Salt and fresh ground pepper

Make the glaze: Put the tequila and sugar in a heavy-bottomed saucepan over medium-high heat. Cook until they are slightly thickened and syrupy and have reduced to approximately ⅔ cup (165 ml), about 5 to 8 minutes. Remove the pan from the heat and add the adobo sauce and minced chipotle.

Make the lamb: Preheat the grill heat to medium-high. Brush the lamb with the olive oil and season it liberally with salt and pepper on all sides. Cover the exposed bones with foil. Grill the lamb with the grill closed for about 6 minutes per side, or until it reaches an internal temperature of 135°F (57°C). Take the lamb off the grill and let it rest for at least 5 minutes before cutting it into individual chops.

Spoon 1 tablespoon of the glaze onto each plate and place a chop on top or serve the glaze in a small bowl beside them.

10-Minute Happy Hour

No time to whip up all the simple syrups and ingredients for this month's complete cocktail club? No worries—you still can have your tequila and a great time, too. Mix up a nice cold Pink Paloma cocktail (page 89) and serve it with a big bowl of tortilla chips and salsa for cocktail club's 10-Minute Happy Hour this month.

Cosmo Slushy, page 104

JULY

chapter 7

FROZEN DRINKS

Perfect for Your Next Staycation

July's heat can bring you to your melting point, which is why it's the perfect time to gather your friends and clink a few frozen cocktails. Classic frozen cocktails such as the Margarita, the Piña Colada, and the Daiquiri pop with unexpected flavors such as prickly pear and watermelon, and with just a couple of tweaks, almost any cocktail can be blended into its frozen counterpart. So get ready to spend some quality time with your blender, icemaker, and even popsicle sticks this month. Let's get to sipping!

Frozen Cocktails Get Interesting

Typically when we think of frozen cocktails, we conjure up images of drinks that have been blended and churned with ice, giving us something we can slurp or eat with a spoon. However, there are other ways to give your cocktails the frozen effect without the use of a blender. Think outside the box and try some of these techniques for adding frozen flair to your drinks this month.

Freeze your fruit juice or mixer. Simply take the non-alcoholic portion of your drink, such as the fruit juice, citrus, and simple syrup, and freeze it into cubes.

Use whole fruit as ice cubes. Most fresh fruit can be frozen on a parchment-lined baking sheet and used instead of ice cubes. Small berries such as raspberries, strawberries, blackberries, cranberries, and blueberries; fruit like grapes and orange, lemon, or lime slices; and vegetables like olives or cocktail onions freeze into gorgeous icy garnishes. You can also cut larger fruit into cubes or ball with a melon baller and freeze in a single layer.

Grab your ice cream scoop. Make a bigger batch (about 4 to 6 servings) of any cocktail and pour this into a freezer-safe baking dish. Freeze it overnight and then use your ice cream scoop to dish up your slushie cocktails the next day. They won't freeze rock solid because of the alcohol content and are best served with small spoons for your guests to enjoy. These slushie scoops look great served in martini glasses.

Make adult snow cones. As with the ice cream scoop method, mix and freeze a larger batch of drinks. After your pan of cocktails has been in the freezer for 45 minutes, use a fork to scrape it and repeat every 30 minutes until you have a pan of shaved icy cocktail. Serve the shaved ice snow-cone style in paper cones or in martini glasses with a tiny spoon.

Make a splash with one giant cube. We've discussed the attributes of using cracked ice, but I just love the look of one giant ice cube in an old-fashioned glass. Look for a giant ice cube tray and make several ahead of time for a stylish way to make your drinks cool.

Smoking cold drinks. Dry ice can also be bought at grocery stores, but typically they keep it in the back, so call ahead to secure your block. Break the block into smaller pieces to fit into a cocktail shaker, then add your drink ingredients and shake. Strain your smoking cold drink into a glass. Don't forget to always wear gloves when handling dry ice and never add it directly to your cocktail glass or it will surely shatter it.

Ice cream. Any creamy cocktails can take a turn in the ice cream machine. This works for wine cocktails, too. Red wine and cracked black pepper sorbet is delicious, and this month's Bourbon Ice Cream (page 106) is a must.

Cocktail in a cube. Freeze your entire cocktail in steps to make one layered cube, using a large ice cube tray or small paper cups. Since alcohol on its own does not freeze well, you need to dilute your alcohol with two parts water before pouring the mixture into your molds to freeze. Let it freeze completely, about 1 hour. Then add your next layer, say fruit juice, and freeze. Continue until you have beautiful striped frozen cocktails. Unmold the cubes and place them in clear glasses. Top with seltzer and serve with a straw.

Pretty perfect infused ice cubes. Herb-, vegetable-, or fruit-infused ice cubes quickly dress up any cocktail. Large pieces of lavender, thyme, or rosemary are beautiful when frozen into cubes, and softer herbs like cilantro and parsley can make a Bloody

Mary even more delicious. If you're looking to add some color to your drinks, cut up kiwi and strawberries for pink and green cubes or go for a burst of blue and add sliced blueberries or blackberries to your ice cubes. For spice, sliced jalapeños and red chiles frozen in cubes add color and heat to cocktails.

PARTY FAVOR

Brain freeze is an intense headache brought on by eating or drinking cold items, and occurs because there is a nerve center at the roof of your mouth that triggers blood vessels to expand and warm the brain to protect it from freezing. You can stop this by pressing your tongue or thumb firmly to the roof of your mouth, or avoid it altogether by taking smaller sips or bites of your frozen treats.

Get Your Drink On!

Get ready to taste some sweet frozen treats, including popsicles, milk shakes, and floats, and some refreshing chilly treats like the Cosmo Slushy (page 104) and the Frozen Prickly Pear Margarita (page 105). Silly straws and drink umbrellas give frozen drinks even more style, so feel free to go ahead and dress up your drinks this month.

Tips for This Month
Before We Get to the Blender
Don't break out the blender just yet; first we have to discuss the ice. In May we talked about cracked ice (page 74) and this month, it's back. Big ice cubes can break a blender before you're even through one batch and shaved ice simply waters down your drinks. So it's a good idea to start cracking some ice ahead of time and fill large zip-top bags and store them in your freezer. Also, if you're the host this month, think about borrowing a couple of extra blenders.

℃ The Classics ℈

PIÑA COLADA

SERVES 1

This rum-based cocktail was made popular in Puerto Rico in 1954 by the bartender Ramon Marrero. Now you can find this stunning sip served all over the world, though it is especially popular on beaches from Jamaica to the Virgin Islands. While it can be served on the rocks, we'll stick with the frozen version this month. So if you like Piña Coladas and getting caught in the rain, bust out your blender and indulge.

3 ounces (90 ml) coconut cream
½ cup (120 ml) pineapple juice
¼ cup (60 ml) white rum

1 cup (240 ml) cracked ice
Pineapple wedge, for garnish
Maraschino cherry, for garnish

In a blender, combine the coconut cream, juice, and rum.

Add the ice and blend until smooth.

Pour the drink into a chilled glass and garnish with the pineapple wedge and cherry.

THE HEMINGWAY DAIQUIRI: PAPA DOBLE STYLE

SERVES 2

The Hemingway Daiquiri, popularly known as a Papa Doble, is a double-sized frozen Daiquiri sans sugar, named for the famed writer Ernest Hemingway.

¼ cup (60 ml) white rum
1 ounce freshly squeezed lime juice
1 tablespoon maraschino cherry liqueur

1 tablespoon grapefruit juice
Lime peel, for garnish
1½ to 2 cups (360 to 480 ml) cracked ice

Add all of the ingredients, except the garnish, to a blender. Start by adding 1 cup of ice, then if you prefer it a little more slushy, add more ice a ½ cup (120 ml) at a time and pulse to blend to your desired consistency. Blend until smooth.

Pour into a glass and garnish with the lime peel. Serve with a straw. If you're craving an original daiquiri, that recipe makes an appearance next month when we dive into rum drinks (see page 117).

✿ New Twists ✿

CHERRY-VANILLA VODKA POPSICLES

For the vanilla simple syrup:
½ cup (100 g) sugar

½ vanilla bean

For the popsicles:
1½ cups (360 ml) tonic water
5 ounces (150 ml) vanilla-flavored vodka
¼ cup (60 ml) vanilla simple syrup

6 ounces (170 g) frozen cherries,
roughly chopped

Make the vanilla simple syrup: Combine the sugar and ½ cup (120 ml) of water in a small saucepan over medium-high heat. Add the vanilla bean. Simmer until all of the sugar is dissolved. Remove the bean, scrape the inside of the bean into the simple syrup, and stir evenly to combine. Pour the syrup into a clean container and let it cool.

Make the popsicles: In a large bowl, mix the tonic, vodka, and syrup together and then fold in the cherries. Pour the mixture into popsicle molds or very small paper cups, like Dixie Cups. If using paper cups, place them filled on a tray and cover the cups with foil. Insert the popsicle sticks through the foil before placing them in the freezer. Freeze overnight.

To release the popsicles from their molds, run the outside of the molds briefly under hot water. Do this ahead of the arrival time of your guests. Fan the popsicles out on a tray and keep them in the freezer until ready to serve.

SPIKED CINNAMON COFFEE MILK SHAKE

SERVES 2

¼ teaspoon ground cinnamon
1 teaspoon honey
1 cup (240 ml) vanilla ice cream, softened

¾ cup (180 ml) brewed strong coffee, cold
½ cup (240 ml) spiced rum
1½ cups (360 ml) cracked ice
2 cinnamon sticks

In a small microwave-safe bowl, combine the cinnamon, honey, and 1 teaspoon of water. Heat for 20 seconds in the microwave to loosen the honey and evenly mix in the cinnamon.

In a blender, combine the honey-cinnamon mixture, ice cream, coffee, rum, and ice and blend until smooth. Divide the milk shake between two glasses. Garnish each with a cinnamon stick and serve.

COSMO SLUSHY

SERVES 3 TO 8 (SEE NOTE)

4½ ounces (135 ml) vodka or citrus vodka   *¼ cup (60 ml) triple sec or Cointreau*
½ cup (240 ml) cranberry juice cocktail   *1½ ounces freshly squeezed lime juice*

In a large freezer-safe container, combine all of the ingredients and stir to mix evenly. Freeze them for 1 hour and then stir again. This will never freeze solid but you will get a great slushy mix. Scoop the slushies into martini or wine glasses and enjoy.

Note: Depending which size scoop you use, this can serve 3 to 4 large scoops or 6 to 8 small scoops.

FROZEN PRICKLY PEAR MARGARITA

SERVES 2 TO 3

You've already read about infusing spirits on page 14, but now you get to try it!

For the infused tequila:
    10 prickly pear fruits, peeled   *1 (750-ml) bottle silver tequila*

For the margaritas:

2 tequila-infused prickly pears (reserved from infusion)
½ cup (240 ml) prickly pear-infused tequila
1½ ounces freshly squeezed lime juice

1½ ounces agave syrup
1½ ounces Cointreau
Cracked ice

Following the instructions for infusing spirits on page 14, completely immerse the peeled prickly pears in the tequila and infuse for 10 to 14 days.

Strain out the tequila and discard all but two of the tequila-infused prickly pears. Mash this through a strainer to remove the fibrous seeds. In a blender, add the mashed prickly pear, infused tequila, lime juice, syrup, and Cointreau. Pulse to combine.

Add 1 to 2 cups ice and blend until smooth. Pour the drinks into margarita glasses and enjoy.

BOURBON–AMARETTO SOUR POPS

MAKES 5 (2-OUNCE/60-ML) POPSICLES

For the lemon-based sour mix (intructions on page 15):

½ cup (100 g) sugar

1 cup (480 ml) freshly squeezed lemon juice

For the pops:

½ cup (240 ml) lemon-based sweet and sour mix
½ cup (240 ml) amaretto

¼ cup (60 ml) bourbon
Maraschino cherries, for garnish

In a large bowl, combine the sour mix, amaretto, and bourbon until evenly mixed. Place a cherry in the bottom of 5 small paper cups or popsicle molds. Pour ¼ cup (60 ml) of the cocktail into each cup. If using paper cups, place the cups on a tray or a plate with a flat surface. Cover them with foil and insert short popsicle sticks. Freeze for 4 hours.

To release the popsicles from their molds, run the outside of the molds briefly under hot water. Do this ahead of the arrival time of your guests. Fan the popsicles out on a tray and keep them in the freezer until ready to serve.

ROOT BEER FLOAT
WITH BOURBON ICE CREAM

SERVES 10 TO 12

2 cups (480 ml) heavy cream
1 cup (240 ml) half-and-half
¾ cup (75 g) sugar
½ vanilla bean

6 large egg yolks
½ cup (120 ml) bourbon
Root beer

In a heavy-bottomed saucepan, bring the cream, half-and-half, sugar, and vanilla bean to a boil.

Put the egg yolks in a large stainless-steel bowl. Add the hot cream mixture a little at a time while whisking continually, until the cream is completely incorporated.

Pour the entire mixture back into the saucepan and heat it over medium-high heat for 1 more minute, stirring constantly. Remove it from the heat and strain the custard into a clean bowl.

Add the bourbon and stir until it is evenly combined.

Cool the custard over an ice bath (a larger bowl full of ice and water) until it is cold to the touch. Freeze the custard in an ice cream machine according to the manufacturer's instructions. Pack it into a freezer-safe container and freeze. This can be made up to a week in advance and stored in the freezer.

Scoop the ice cream into small cordial glasses and top them with root beer.

Note: If you don't have an ice cream machine but want to indulge in this frozen treat, use high-quality vanilla ice cream and add 1 ounce of bourbon to your glass, then top with root beer.

Eat Up!

It's not summer without frozen drinks and a blazing barbecue. These simple bites scream summertime, and make for all sorts of adventures in tasting.

JALAPEÑO CORNBREAD
WITH CAYENNE-HONEY BUTTER

MAKES 17 TO 18 MINI MUFFINS

½ cup (1 stick/115 g) unsalted butter,
    softened
2 tablespoons honey
⅛ teaspoon cayenne pepper
Pinch of salt
Cooking spray

1 (8½-ounce/240-g) box cornbread
    muffin mix
⅓ cup (75 ml) whole milk
1 large egg
2 tablespoons minced fresh jalapeño

Preheat the oven to 400°F (205°C). Coat a 24-serving mini muffin tin with cooking spray (some of the cups will be empty).

In a small bowl, combine the butter, honey, cayenne, and salt. Place the butter in the middle of a large sheet of plastic wrap, fold the plastic wrap over the butter, and form into a log the diameter of a quarter, wrapping all sides and squeezing in the ends like a piece of wrapped candy. Chill the butter until hard, then cut it into 18 thin pats to serve alongside the muffins.

In a medium bowl, stir the muffin mix, milk, egg, and jalapeño until well mixed. Evenly divide the batter into 17 or 18 muffin tins, filling each cup about three-quarters full.

Bake the muffins until golden, about 10 to 12 minutes. Remove and allow them to cool for 10 minutes before removing them from the pan. Serve warm with the cayenne-honey butter.

Note: If you would like your muffins on the spicier side, feel free to add more minced jalapeño to the muffin mix or more cayenne to the butter.

GRILLED BRIE
WITH HONEY-BARBECUE SAUCE

SERVES 10 TO 12

1 (4-inch/10-cm) wheel Brie, rind intact
  (see Note)
½ cup (120 ml) barbecue sauce

¼ cup (60 ml) honey
Crackers or baguette toasts, for serving

Preheat a grill to cook over direct medium-high heat. Take the Brie from the refrigerator cold and grill it for about 4 to 7 minutes on each side, until it gets grill marks.

In a small microwave-safe bowl, heat the barbecue sauce and honey together for 30 seconds in the microwave and mix to combine them evenly. Drizzle the honey-barbecue sauce on a platter. Place the Brie on top of the sauce. Serve the cheese with a knife and crackers or grilled baguette slices.

Note: Do not trim the rind of your cheese. You want the entire white-washed rind fully intact to keep all of the melted cheese inside as you grill it.

GRILLED PINEAPPLE
WITH CHILI, LIME, AND COCONUT

SERVES 10 TO 12

2 tablespoons finely shredded unsweetened
  coconut
1 teaspoon lime zest

1 pineapple, peeled, cored, and cut into
  ½-inch (12-mm)-thick rounds
Cooking spray
½ teaspoon chili powder

Toast the coconut in a dry small sauté pan over medium heat. Stir frequently until the coconut begins to brown and becomes fragrant, about 6 to 8 minutes. Stir together the coconut and zest in a bowl and set aside.

Preheat a grill to cook over direct medium-high heat. Spray each side of the sliced pineapple with cooking spray. Grill each side for 2 minutes.

Evenly sprinkle the grilled pineapple slices with the chili powder and the toasted coconut–lime zest mixture. Serve immediately.

10-Minute Happy Hour

It's frozen drink month, so if you only have 10 minutes, buzz up a batch of Piña Coladas (page 102)! Simply serve them alongside some sliced watermelon for a perfect happy hour to end a hot summer's day.

Queen's Rum Shaker, page 118

AUGUST

chapter 8

RUM

The Original American Spirit

Rum has a long-storied and, at times, sordid past. This is the first spirit Americans consumed in the colonies and over the years rum has been associated with everything from piracy and the slave trade to bad-boy historical figures like Al Capone and Ernest Hemingway. From the light and fruity to the dark and spicy, rum has some equally famous cocktails for us to explore this month. Whether you're hosting cocktail club poolside or planning a tiki-inspired evening, rum cocktails are just what the bartender ordered!

Name Game

While rum is associated mainly with warm locales in the Caribbean, it's also produced in France, Canada, Japan, and Australia. Rum is a distilled spirit made from molasses or sugarcane juice, but styles can vary by proof, aging, and even name: English-speaking countries call it *rum*, the Spanish call it *ron*, and if it's from the French-speaking provinces, it's *rhum*. Unlike other spirits, rum distillers do not have to follow certain regulations, so rum production varies from location to location.

Rum Guide

Rum's color often indicates how it will taste. The lighter colored or colorless rums are typically lighter in body and drier. The darker rums are richer and typically sweeter, with aromas and flavors to match their color. For instance, a golden-hued rum may taste like caramel and vanilla and a black rum will have even richer molasses flavors and aromas. From light and white to dark and spiced, here are the basic variations of rum.

Light or White: Sometimes called silver, this type is clear, light-bodied, and not sweet. Kind of like vodkas, they are almost flavorless and work great in all sorts of cocktails. Spanish-speaking countries such as Cuba, Puerto Rico, Venezuela, the Dominican Republic, Guatemala, and the U.S. Virgin Islands produce white rum along with *ron añejo* (aged rum) and *ron viejo* (old rum), which are typically smooth, more refined rums. Popular brands include Bacardi and Ron Zacapa.

Gold, Oro, or Ambre (a.k.a. amber): These are medium-bodied and generally aged in oak barrels. They can either get their gold tinge from the barrels or from added coloring. They have more color, aroma, and flavor than the light or white rums.

PARTY FAVOR

"Rum Runner" is the name of a cocktail, but it's also a synonym for bootlegging, which is the making, selling, and transporting of illegal alcohol. The one difference is that a bootlegger conducted business on dry land and a rum runner smuggled their booze over water. Perhaps the most famous rum runner was William Frederick McCoy. As legend goes, while many bootleggers watered down their goods, William was known for selling uncut high-quality spirits, earning his product the moniker "The Real McCoy."

Dark or Black: These are aged in charred barrels, which impart all sorts of complex flavors and aromas into the spirit. This also darkens it, though caramel coloring is often added as well. Darker rum is usually more molasses-like in flavor too, meaning it is sweeter and more syrupy than white or light rum. Spots like Grenada, Barbados, Guyana, Trinidad and Tobago, and Jamaica pour up richer, thicker, darker styles of rum. Popular brands include Mount Gay, Cruzan, Appleton, Myer's Dark, and Gosling's Black Seal.

Flavored Rum: Like vodka, these flavored spirits are gaining in popularity at the bar. Flavored rums are typically light or white rums that have been infused with tropical flavors such as coconut, citrus, banana, or mango. Malibu is a popular example.

Spiced Rum: Spiced rums smell and taste like the spices that they are infused with before bottling, and are darker in color. Typically you'll taste cinnamon, anise, nutmeg, vanilla, and toffee. Captain Morgan is among the most popular.

Overproof Rum: These are very high-proof pours. Most commercial rum comes off the still between 160 and 190 proof and then is watered down to between 80 and 100 proof. Overproof rum is bottled at the concentration it comes off the still, and Bacardi 151 and Cruzan Aged Rum 151 are two examples.

Premium: These are rums that are considered special due to the craftsmanship or the age. Like a good Scotch, these are priced accordingly and meant for sipping, not the cocktail shaker. Popular pours are Appleton Estate 30 Year Old, Don Q Gran Añejo, and Ron Zacapa.

Then Came Cachaça

This little Brazilian pour has been popping up on cocktail menus around the globe, and is making an appearance in our Caipirinha this month. Like rum, it is a sugarcane-based spirit, but this one can only be made from distilled pressed fresh sugarcane juice, whereas most rum is made from both sugarcane and a molasses by-product. Cachaça also goes by the name "Brazilian rum."

Taste Test

This month, we are pitting the Mojito (page 115) against the Caipirinha (see the sidebar on page 115). The Mojito is the most beloved Cuban cocktail and the Caipirinha shares that same acclaim with Brazilians. While the Caipirinha has come to be known as the Mojito's Brazilian cousin, there are a few key differences. While both are laden with lime juice and similar spirits, the Caipirinha showcases cachaça and the Mojito calls for rum and adds a little muddled mint and a splash of soda. Make one of each and let your cocktail club choose where their loyalties lie.

Swizzle The "Swizzle" is an entire category of drinks, all made with ice and rum and blended with a swizzle stick. In fact, Bermuda's national drink is the Rum Swizzle! This drink category gets its name from a nineteenth-century island tool that actually looks more like a prehistoric instrument than the pink flamingo-topped swizzle sticks of today. A precursor to the immersion blender, the old-fashioned swizzle was a long (about 15 inches/38 cm), thin branch of hardwood that ended in a fork of three to five prongs used to mix and froth ingredients. Although they're very different looking and much less functional, the swizzle sticks of today—along with drink umbrellas and fun straws—are all part of the cocktail culture of rum drinks and, of course, the best tiki parties.

Rum Culture Rum has a widely-celebrated entertaining culture, so this month, you may just want to add a theme to cocktail club in honor of rum's varied history. Serve up some Mai Tais or Daiquiris with umbrellas for a tiki-inspired soiree or set up your very own speakeasy with a large helping of Prohibition Punch for a roaring good tasting!

❦ Get Your Drink On! ❧

This month, we have both light rum cocktails, like the Queen's Rum Shaker (page 118), which is a delicious summery sip perfect for a portable happy hour, and we taste the darker side of rum with the Dark & Stormy (below). You'll also find some delicious classic cocktails to choose from such as the Mai Tai, the original Daiquiri, and our taste-test stars the Mojito and the Caipirinha. Happy tasting!

Tips for This Month

Gather up highballs, mason jars, and brandy snifters for our cocktails this month. If you plan on doing a daiquiri, try to secure a blender or two, and make sure to stock up on some darling umbrellas and festive swizzle sticks.

❦ The Classics ❧

DARK & STORMY

SERVES 1

Ice cubes
¼ cup (60 ml) dark rum

3 ounces (90 ml) ginger beer
1 tablespoon freshly squeezed lime juice

In a tall glass full of ice, stir together all of the ingredients.

MOJITO

SERVES 1

1 ounce simple syrup (page 15), or 1
    teaspoon superfine sugar
1½ teaspoons freshly squeezed lime juice
6 to 8 fresh mint leaves, plus a sprig for
    garnish

¼ cup (60 ml) white rum
Ice cubes
Club soda

Add the simple syrup, lime juice, and mint to a glass and muddle them lightly, just to release those minty good aromas. Add the rum and fill the glass with ice. Stir. Top it off with club soda and add a sprig of mint.

SHAKE IT UP

- Remove the mint leaves and use cachaça in place of white rum and you've got a Caipirinha.
- Remove the simple syrup and subtitute coconut rum for a Cojito.

MAI TAI

SERVES 1

This is a must if you're feeling tiki this month. The kitschy Cali-Polynesian–inspired restaurant Trader Vic's was credited with this creation in the 1940s, but another bartender named Don the Beachcomber may have gotten there first back in the 1930s (like most cocktail lore, details are a little fuzzy). Regardless of its origins, one sip of the fruity Mai Tai will have you transported from your kitchen to the white sandy beaches of Hawaii in an instant. Garnish with a colorful drink umbrella for the full experience.

Ice cubes
¼ cup (60 ml) dark rum
1 ounce fresh lime juice

1 ounce orgeat syrup (see Note)
1 tablespoon orange curaçao

Combine all of the ingredients in a shaker filled with ice and shake until chilled. Serve in a tall glass.

Note: Orgeat syrup is an almond-flavored sweetened syrup. You can buy orgeat syrup online or at some grocery stores that have syrups for flavoring "gourmet" coffee drinks. Torani is a widely available brand.

FROZEN STRAWBERRY DAIQUIRI

The original daiquiri is attributed to American Jennings Cox, who was the first to whip it up in Daiquiri, Cuba. Usually reserved for cocktails whose ingredients are rum, lime juice, and sugar, most daiquiris now include fruit and can be served frozen or on the rocks like the original. Ripe strawberries are usually sweet enough for this version, however if yours aren't quite ripe, you can add a little simple syrup.

3 cups (430 g) fresh strawberries, hulled
and roughly chopped
1 cup (240 ml) white rum

¼ cup (60 ml) freshly squeezed lime juice
Ice cubes

Combine the strawberries, rum, and lime juice in a blender. Depending on how thick you want your frozen daiquiris, you can add as much or as little ice as desired. Start with 1 cup (240 ml). Then if you prefer it a little more slushy, add more ice a ½ cup (120 ml) at a time and pulse to blend to your desired consistency.

Divide the daiquiri between glasses and serve.

SHAKE IT UP

Add 1½ ounces white rum, 1 ounce simple syrup, and 1½ teaspoons freshly squeezed lime juice to the shaker, and pour over ice for an original daiquiri.

New Twists

PROHIBITION PUNCH

SERVES 1

Rum punch has about as many varieties as rum itself. The retro drink list at my favorite Grand Central Station bar, The Campbell Apartment, in New York City is full of throwbacks and nods to the past, with popular sips like this Prohibition Punch. Served in an enormous glass, slightly smaller than a fish bowl, this drink is icy cold, refreshing, and the perfect place for some good rum. We'll taste the beloved Caribbean Bajan Rum Punch next month (page 127).

¼ cup (60 ml) passion fruit juice
1 ounce Appelton Estate Rum V/X (see
Note)
1 tablespoon Grand Marnier

Splash cranberry juice
Splash freshly squeezed lemon juice
Ice cubes
1 ounce Moët & Chandon Champagne

In a large brandy snifter, combine the rum, Grand Marnier, and fruit juices with a lots of ice, and stir to chill. Top with the Champagne right before enjoying.

Note: The Appleton Estate V/X is a Jamaican gold rum full of delicious flavors like orange peel, spices, and brown sugar.

QUEEN'S RUM SHAKER

SERVES 1

Making cocktails in mason jars that come with fitted lids is the ideal way to take happy hour on the go, as you can see on page 110. Instead of bringing an appetizer to your next party, whip these up and offer to bring the drinks!

> 6 fresh mint leaves
> 1 ounce simple syrup (page 15)
> 1 ounce freshly squeezed lime juice
> 1/3 cup (75 ml) white rum
> 6 dashes of Angostura bitters
> Ice cubes
> Mint sprigs, for garnish

Put the mint leaves into a mason jar with the simple syrup and lime juice. Using a muddler or wooden spoon, gently mix together and bruise the mint leaves.

Add the rum and bitters. Place the lid on the jar securely until you are safely at your destination. Once you have arrived, add ice and place the lid back on securely. Shake vigorously to chill. Remove the lid, add a sprig of mint and a straw, and enjoy.

Eat Up!

Jerk chicken serves up a kick that's just right alongside some of this month's more refreshing rum sips like the Mojito (page 115) and the Queen's Rum Shaker (above) to tame their heat. Summer's juicy little tomatoes and sweet ripe peaches complete the menu and are perfect when paired with an icy glass of Prohibition Punch (page 117).

JERK CHICKEN
WITH PINEAPPLE AND RUM GLAZE

SERVES 8 TO 12

For the pineapple:

1 (8-ounce/225-g) can crushed pineapple, drained (reserve juice)

2 scallions, chopped (about 2 tablespoons)

For the Jamaican Jerk Spice Rub:

1 tablespoon plus 1½ teaspoons dark brown sugar

1 teaspoon salt

1 teaspoon ground coriander

½ teaspoon dried thyme

½ teaspoon allspice

½ teaspoon onion powder

½ teaspoon cinnamon

½ teaspoon cayenne pepper (you can use less if you want it less spicy)

Few grinds of black pepper

For the chicken:

2 boneless, skinless chicken breasts

1 tablespoon Jamaican jerk spice rub, homemade or store-bought

Olive oil, for grilling

3 to 4 scallions cut into 1½-inch (4-cm) pieces

For the glaze:

¼ cup (60 ml) spiced rum

¼ cup (50 g) packed dark brown sugar

¼ cup (60 ml) reserved pineapple juice

Pinch of salt

Make the pineapple: Stir together the crushed pineapple and chopped scallions and set aside.

Make the chicken: Combine all of the jerk spice rub ingredients in a small bowl. Evenly coat the chicken with the jerk spice rub and refrigerate for 1 to 2 hours.

When you are ready to cook, preheat a grill to cook over direct medium-high heat. Brush the chicken breasts with a little oil and grill for about 6 to 7 minutes per side, or until the internal temperature reaches 170°F (77°C). Remove them from the grill to rest for 5 to 10 minutes.

Make the glaze: Combine all of the ingredients in a small pot and bring them to a boil. Reduce the heat and allow the glaze to reduce until it has thickened to a syrupy consistency, about 8 to 10 minutes.

When you are ready to serve, cut the chicken into bite-sized chunks. On small skewers or tooth-picks, thread 1 piece of scallion, then 1 piece of chicken. Serve the skewers with the rum glaze and pineapple on the side to dip into.

Note: For spicier bites, cut the raw chicken into bite-sized chunks, then toss the pieces in the spice rub. Cook them in 2 teaspoons oil in a large cast-iron pan for about 6 to 8 minutes.

HEIRLOOM TOMATOES, BASIL, AND MOZZARELLA WITH A BALSAMIC DRIZZLE

SERVES 8 TO 12

1 large heirloom tomato, cut into 1-inch (2.5-cm) chunks
8 ounces (225 g) small fresh mozzarella balls
24 fresh basil leaves

2 tablespoons store-bought balsamic glaze
2 tablespoons good-quality extra-virgin olive oil
Salt
Fresh ground black pepper

Thread 1 chunk of tomato, 1 mozzarella ball, and 1 basil leaf on small skewers. Drizzle with the glaze and oil and season with salt and pepper. Serve immediately.

Note: If you can't find balsamic glaze, you can make your own. Put 1 cup (240 ml) balsamic vinegar in a small pot over medium heat and bring it to a smimmer. Reduce it to 1/4 cup (60 ml), about 20 to 25 minutes. Use 2 tablespoons for this recipe and save the remainder for another use.

PEACHES AND PROSCIUTTO

SERVES 16

4 ounces (115 g) walnuts, chopped fine
4 ounces (115 g) almonds, chopped fine
4 ounces (115 g) soft blue cheese

4 ripe peaches, pitted and sliced into thin wedges
8 slices prosciutto, cut in half lengthwise
Fresh ground black pepper

Combine the almonds and walnuts in a bowl and set them aside.

Use a wooden spoon to beat the blue cheese in a bowl to soften it. Press the cheese onto the peaches with a knife, or place thin slices on each peach wedge. Then press the finely chopped nuts into the cheese.

Roll each peach slice in a piece of prosciutto. Top the peaches with pepper and serve chilled.

10-Minute Happy Hour

This month's abbreviated cocktail club takes on a new twist with the Queen's Rum Shaker (page 118). It's simple to whip up and perfect for cocktails to go. Pick up some cheeses, fruit, and a loaf of fresh bread and take these portable cocktails on the road. Whether you're picnicking or just headed to a friend's, this food and drink combo makes for a stellar happy hour in no time.

Sparking Cucumber Honeydew
Sangria and Radishes with Herb
Butter and Salt, pages 129 and 132

SEPTEMBER

chapter 9

SANGRIA & PITCHER DRINKS

Pitcher Perfect

Pitcher drinks like Sangria are super popular and for good reason: Your choice of flavors, fruits, type of wine, and other ingredients are endless. This month, bigger is better. From your garden to your grocery store, to your wine purveyor and back home again, we'll be building big batches of all sorts of sips, from punch to a Spiked Iced Soy Chai Tea. Break out grandma's punch bowl—it's time to give that thing another go.

All Hail Sangria

Sangria is the most popular pitcher drink on the planet. With the rise in popularity of tapas restaurants, not to mention the influx of mouthwatering images online, these pretty pitchers continue to win over newcomers. The traditional red wine version has undergone multiple makeovers, giving us every possible flavor combination to choose from. Far from the sickly sweet concoctions of the past, great Sangria can be a refreshing addition to any party.

These days, even serious craft cocktail bars are stirring up batches of Sangria incorporating top-shelf liquors like tequila and rum, high-end wines from Viognier to Champagne, and all sorts of flavors like ginger and jalapeño (you can even make delicious non-alcoholic sangrias). There's a Sangria out there for everyone—even you.

How to Make a Signature Sangria

If you know the basics of Sangria, the sky is the limit. There are no strict guidelines here, so have fun mixing and matching with these basic ingredients:

- Wine of your choice. Start with one standard 750-ml bottle.
- Sliced fruit/s or whole berries. I recommend starting with 1½ cups (340 g).
- A spirit, traditionally brandy, but vodka, rum, and tequila work too. Start with ½ cup (120 ml).
- A sweet element. You can add sugar, ¼ cup (60 ml) fruit juice, or 3 ounces (90 ml) of a sweet spirit like Cointreau, triple sec, or Grand Marnier.
- Some spritz, like ginger ale or club soda. They come in at the end to top off the pitcher.

Now that you know the basics, try your hand at switching up the fruit/herb/wine combinations with the guide below and you're sure to find a Sangria perfect for you:

- Apples, mint, un-oaked Chardonnay
- Mixed berry, jalapeño, Viognier
- White peach, basil, Moscato
- Peach, thyme, Pinot Noir
- Strawberry, mint, sparkling wine
- Honeydew, mint, Pinot Grigio
- Strawberry, basil, Chardonnay
- Blood orange, lemon thyme, sparkling wine
- Cherry, rosemary, Syrah

- Stone fruit (plums, cherries, peaches), mint, Pinot Noir
- Raspberry, thyme, Rosé
- Blackberry, basil, Pinot Grigio
- Pineapple, ginger, Albariño
- Blackberry, ginger, Cabernet
- Pineapple, lemon balm, Moscato
- Cucumber, ginger, sparkling wine
- Lychee, raspberry, sake
- Kiwi, strawberry, basil, Sauvignon Blanc

While traditional Sangria calls for brandy, or sometimes brandy and curaçao, you should experiment with switching up the alcoholic ingredients, too. Rum works with tropical fruits and a light white wine. Tequila loves citrus, so think lemons, limes, and Sauvignon Blanc. Gin works great with lemons and limes, even melon or cucumbers, and the Portuguese light white wine Vinho Verde. Or substitute lemonade or white cranberry juice for all of the alcoholic ingredients for an alcohol-free sip!

Taste Test

This month you can taste test how switching just one ingredient dramatically alters the final pour. Serve up one batch of the Raspberry and Thyme Rosé Pitcher (page 130), as the recipe is written and then serve up another batch swapping out the dry pink Rosé with another pink wine—White Zinfandel, for example. Even though these two wines may look exactly the same, they are dramatically different. The White Zinfandel will make a much sweeter sangria. See which one your cocktail club likes best.

The Rules for Bottled and Prebatched Drinks

The ease and enjoyment offered by premaking a cocktail isn't just for entertaining at home. In fact, even swanky cocktail spots are enjoying the ease of prebatched cocktails, because they lessen the wait time for customers and give the bartender a little breathing room from the constant looming line of thirsty patrons.

Popular prebatched cocktails include the French 75 (page 163), the Corpse Reviver #2 (page 156), and the Negroni (page 27). Like any big-batch drinks, serving up fresh is best, but that doesn't necessarily mean they need to be made à la carte. Here is a timeline for prebatching some popular pours:

- *A few days before:* Drinks with only liquor ingredients, like the Martini, the Negroni, or the Manhattan.
- *The night before:* Drinks with sliced fruit, like Sangria. In fact, some prefer to pre-batch so that the sliced fruit and spirits have time to infuse.
- *The morning of:* Cocktails with prepared or freshly squeezed fruit juice, like Margaritas or Pink Palomas.
- *Last minute:* Any cocktail with a spritzy ingredient, whether it's seltzer or Champagne, cannot be completely prebatched. You can, however, just add the spritz to a bottled cocktail right before serving; just place a little note on it in the fridge so you don't forget to add the last ingredient.

Big Ice is Better

For pitcher drinks, large whole cubes—not cracked, crushed, or shaved—are best. If you're planning on serving in a punch bowl, think even bigger! Find a small freezer-safe bowl that can fit into your punch bowl, fill it with water, and stir in any fruit, herb, or edible flower garnish you'd like. Freeze this overnight. Once you have assembled your drink ingredients in the punch bowl, remove the bowl of ice from the freezer. Run the bottom and sides under warm water to loosen the ice, and turn it out into the punch bowl. This block should last for hours in a shady spot.

PARTY FAVOR

Originally, punch was served in small glasses to encourage guests to return to the punch bowl multiple times throughout an event, the belief being that it sparks conversation and makes for a merry soiree. Consider scaling down the size of your glassware next time you offer up punch or pitcher drinks and see if you notice a difference.

❧ Get Your Drink On! ☙

Big-batch drinks can be a host or hostess's best friend. Prebatching, or making these in advance, frees you up to mingle. It's also great for entertaining a variety of people, since it's easy enough to throw together a quick, and even kid-friendly, punch. Punch bowls and pitcher drinks are also the ultimate elegant and functional centerpieces. With all of that beautiful fruit and sparkling ice in one pretty pitcher, all eyes will be on those drinks. For cocktail club this month, try to set up stations if you have the space. Place your pitchers in different serving areas to create a smooth flow and multiple conversation areas.

Tips for This Month

It may seem like this month you can throw anything in a bowl, pour in some wine and booze, and voilá—you have a punch. But a little more finesse is required for these beautiful drinks to taste as good as they look:

- *Plan ahead.* Pitcher drinks and punch should not be a catch-all for your leftovers and half-full bottles lingering on the bar.
- *Use what's in season.* See which fruits and herbs are at their peak when you're out shopping and let this guide your drink recipes. Just as with infused spirits, bitters, and tinctures, a higher-proof base spirit will pull more flavor out of your fruit.
- *Let the recipe be a guide, not a requirement.* Be adventurous and try swapping out different ingredients using the guide on page 124.
- *Follow the tips for bottled and prebatched drinks* (page 125) to see which pitchers you can make ahead of time.
- *Taste-test every batch.* Treat big batches just as you would a singular carefully crafted cocktail, and tread lightly when sweetening. Just as you finish dishes by seasoning with salt and pepper, you should always tweak the sweetness or tartness of your drinks before serving.

❧ The Classics ☙

MILK PUNCH

SERVES 6

This vintage pour is a New Orleans favorite.

¾ cup (180 ml) brandy
¾ cup (180 ml) dark rum
¼ cup (60 ml) simple syrup (page 15)

12 dashes of vanilla extract
3 cups (720 ml) whole milk
Freshly grated nutmeg (optional)

In a pitcher ¾ filled with ice, combine all of the ingredients and stir until evenly mixed. Pour into ice-filled glasses and top with grated nutmeg for garnish.

BAJAN RUM PUNCH

SERVES 6

The jingle for easily remembering this famous big batch punch from Barbados goes like this: "One of Sour, Two of Sweet, Three of Strong, and Four of Weak." That is: one part lime juice, two parts sweetener, three parts rum, and four parts water.

3 ounces (90 ml) freshly squeezed lime juice
¾ cup (180 ml) simple syrup (page 15)
9 ounces (270 ml) dark Bajan rum
*   (the older, the better)*

1½ cups (360 ml) water
12 dashes of Angostura bitters
Freshly grated nutmeg (optional)

Stir all ingredients together in a large pitcher and pour over ice.

TRADITIONAL SANGRIA

SERVES 6

1 lemon, sliced into rounds
½ orange, slice into rounds
1 apple, cored and sliced
1 lime, sliced into rounds
1 (750-ml) bottle Spanish red wine
*   (such as Rioja)*

¼ cup (60 ml) Cointreau
½ cup (120 ml) brandy
3 ounces (90 ml) freshly squeezed
*   orange juice*
2 cups (480 ml) club soda (ginger ale
*   if you want it sweeter)*

In a large pitcher, add the fruit first, then the wine, spirits, and orange juice. Stir and refrigerate it overnight. Add the club soda just before serving and serve over ice.

New Twists

SPARKLING WHITE PEACH SANGRIA

SERVES 4 TO 6

2 large or 3 small white peaches, sliced
¾ cup (180 ml) peach brandy
1 (750-ml) bottle Moscato, chilled

4½ cups (1 L) white peach seltzer water,
*   chilled*
Ice cubes

Put three-quarters of the sliced peaches and the brandy in a pitcher and lightly muddle the peaches. Add the Moscato and seltzer. Stir with a wooden spoon to mix. Pour the sangria into ice-filled glasses and top with a couple of fresh peach slices.

From left: Sparkling Cucumber and Honeydew Sangria, Blueberry-Lavender Vodka Spritzer, and Radishes with Herb Butter and Salt

SPARKLING CUCUMBER AND
HONEYDEW SANGRIA

SERVES 4 TO 6

1 cup (225 g) thinly sliced cucumber
1 cup (225 g) cubed honeydew
½ cup (120 ml) Hendrick's gin
¼ cup (60 ml) curaçao

1 (750-ml) bottle Cava (Spanish sparkling
* wine), chilled*
1 lemon, thinly sliced
Mint sprigs, for garnish

In a large pitcher, add the cucumber, honeydew, gin, and curaçao. Lightly muddle the cucumber and melon.

Add the Cava and lemon and stir lightly. Scoop some of the cucumber and melon from the pitcher into each glass. Top with ice, pour in the sangria, and garnish with a sprig of mint.
Serve immediately.

Note: This sangria can be made spicy with the addition of one small jalapeño pepper, sliced into rounds with the seeds removed.

BLUEBERRY-LAVENDER VODKA SPRITZER

SERVES 6 TO 8

1 cup (225 g) fresh blueberries
2 cups (480 ml) vodka
¾ cup (180 ml) blueberry-lavender simple
* syrup (recipe follows)*

½ cup (120 ml) freshly squeezed lime juice
3 cups (720 ml) club soda
Fresh lavender, for garnish

Make blueberry ice in one of two ways: Either divide the blueberries between two ice cube trays and fill them with water or spread the berries evenly on a baking sheet and freeze them until solid.

In a large glass pitcher, combine the vodka, blueberry-lavender simple syrup, lime juice, and club soda. Add about half of the blueberry ice cubes or frozen blueberries and divide the remaining half among the glasses. Pour the drink mixture over top and serve each with a sprig of lavender.

BLUEBERRY-LAVENDER SIMPLE SYRUP

1 cup (200 g) sugar
1 cup (225 g) fresh blueberries

4 fresh lavender sprigs, or 1½ teaspoons
* dried food-grade lavender*

Combine 1 cup (240 ml) of water, the sugar, and blueberries in a saucepan and bring them to a boil, stirring to dissolve the sugar. Reduce the heat to low and add the lavender; simmer for 10 minutes. Strain the syrup into a clean container, pressing the blueberries to get all of their juice. Store in an airtight container in the refrigerator for up to 2 weeks.

SPIKED ICED SOY CHAI TEA

SERVES 6

4 to 6 spiced or black chai tea bags, or 8
   teaspoons loose tea
1 cup (240 ml) vanilla soy milk

1 cup (240 ml) aged rum (bourbon or white
   rum may be substituted)
Honey or agave syrup (optional)

Combine the tea bags and 2 quarts (2 L) of cold water in a large pitcher and cover. If you are using loose leaves, a large French press for tea works great. Place the mixture in the refrigerator overnight, or at least 8 hours. The longer you leave the tea to cold brew, the stronger it will become.

Remove the tea bags. Add the soy milk and rum and stir to combine. If your soy milk is unsweetened, you can add a bit of sweetener to taste. Serve over ice.

RASPBERRY AND THYME ROSÉ PITCHER

SERVES 4 TO 6

Replacing processed ingredients with natural add-ins like muddled raspberries and fresh thyme, this pitcher is not your typical sugar-laden harbinger of a hangover. For a spritzier sip with less body, try substituting Prosecco for the Rosé.

¼ cup (55 g) granulated sugar
¼ cup (60 ml) framboise
1½ cups (340 g) fresh raspberries

1 (750-ml) bottle dry Rosé wine, chilled
Ice cubes
6 sprigs fresh thyme, washed, for garnish

Bring the sugar and 1 cup (240 ml) of water to a simmer in a small saucepan, stirring just until the sugar is dissolved. In a pitcher, pour this syrup and the framboise over the raspberries and let them stand for 5 minutes.

Add the wine and stir well. Chill the drink covered until ready to serve. Serve it over ice with a sprig of fresh thyme as garnish.

Eat Up!

Figs are in season right now, so don't miss out! They have the ideal sweetness to stand up to some of our sweeter sips this month. Think you're not a fig fan? Try these bites—one covered in salty prosciutto warm off the grill, the other paired with feta and drizzled with honey and nuts—and I promise you'll become a die-hard fig fan after one taste. On the flip side, we've got radishes fresh from the garden, served in the classic French preparation, with some soft herb butter and crunchy salt for a lighter bite that's lovely alongside this month's spritzy sips.

Blueberry-Lavender
Vodka Spritzer, page 129

RADISHES
WITH HERB BUTTER AND SALT

SERVES 10 TO 12

Trim the radish greens, but leave a bit attached to use as a handle to help in dipping them.

½ cup (1 stick/115 g) good-quality
　unsalted butter, softened (see Note)
1 teaspoon chopped fresh tarragon
1 teaspoon chopped fresh scallions
1 teaspoon freshly squeezed lemon juice
½ teaspoon chopped fresh dill

½ teaspoon chopped fresh parsley
½ teaspoon lemon zest
Fresh ground pepper
About 24 standard or French-style
　breakfast radishes
2 tablespoons good-quality sea salt

In a small bowl, combine the softened butter, tarragon, scallions, lemon juice, dill, parsley, zest, and pepper.

Serve the radishes with the herb butter and a side dish of sea salt. You can either spread the butter on split radishes or simply use the radish to scoop a little butter from the bowl, then sprinkle with sea salt and enjoy.

Note: If you need to soften your butter in a hurry, try cutting the stick into smaller pieces, then place it in a zip-top bag and pound it with a rolling pin. Use your hands to massage it a little; the warmth of your hands will help soften it. Then scrape it back into the bowl and finish working it with a wooden spoon.

GRILLED FIGS WITH PROSCIUTTO

SERVES 12

12 fresh figs, stemmed and cut in half
12 pieces prosciutto, cut in half lengthwise

3 tablespoons olive oil

Preheat a grill to cook over direct medium-low heat. Wrap each fig half with a strip of prosciutto. Brush all the figs with the oil and grill them for 2 to 4 minutes, or until they are warmed through and the prosciutto starts to get crispy.

FRESH FIGS
WITH FETA, MINT, AND HONEY

SERVES 12

24 ($\frac{1}{2}$-inch/12-mm) cubes feta (about 8
   ounces/225 g)
$\frac{1}{4}$ cup (55 g) thinly sliced fresh mint
24 fresh figs, stemmed

$\frac{1}{4}$ cup (60 ml) honey
$\frac{3}{4}$ cup (170 g) toasted hazelnuts, chopped
   fine (you can use almonds, macadamia
   nuts, or walnuts as a substitute)

In a small bowl, toss the feta with the mint. Score each fig at the stem end with an X. Place 1 cube of cheese in each fig.

Microwave the honey for 10 seconds. Drizzle it on each fig and sprinkle them with the nuts. Serve at room temperature.

10-Minute Happy Hour

This month, we're jumping on the fan wagon of Moscato, the slightly sweet and slightly spritzy white wine from the northeastern region of Italy. Mix up a batch of Sparkling White Peach Sangria (page 127) and pair it with some prosciutto-wrapped melon for a pitcher-perfect happy hour in 10 minutes' time.

Kentucky Ginger, page 142

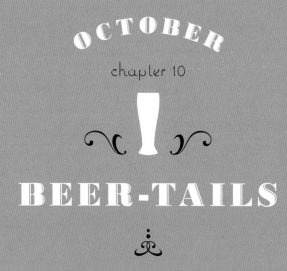

OCTOBER

chapter 10

BEER-TAILS

Beer Takes a Turn in the Shaker

Since October is the time of year for camping and tailgating, beer drinks are the perfect go-to this month. Technically, mixed drinks made with beer instead of a spirit don't qualify as cocktails, but I felt it was a category we couldn't miss. They don't require many mixers or fancy glassware, and this is the one (and only!) time I'll say it's OK to try some of these in a plastic cup. Through vigorous taste testing, I've decided the nuances of some of these drinks are not lost to a plastic tumbler, but my first choice for sipping is always a nice tall beer glass or cocktail glass when appropriate.

Like any of our previous spirits, once you go in search of suitable cocktails, you'll be floored by how many beer cocktails, a.k.a. beer-tails or ale-tails, actually exist. Fans of beer cocktails definitely take the prize for most humorous names. From the Skip & Go Naked (a gin, beer, and sour mix concoction) to the amusing Beer-a-Lade (a recipe of beer, Gatorade, Tobasco sauce, and … maple syrup?), I've seen and tasted it all when it comes to beer cocktails, and hand picked a delicious selection worthy of cocktail club this month.

Brew School: Beer is so much simpler to conquer than most distilled spirits when it comes to mixing cocktails. The categories are more clearly defined, and once you understand the flavors and personalities of each, you'll have a good grasp on how to mix them up into delicious drinks.

Beer is an alcoholic beverage produced from four main ingredients: grain, water, yeast, and hops.

- **Grains** typically used are malted barley and wheat, but other grains such as oats, corn, rice, and rye are used on a much smaller scale. Flavoring ingredients such as fruit and spices can also be added. Beer's color can range from golden tinged to black, and its taste can range from sweet to extremely bitter depending on how long its grains are roasted.
- **Hops** are viney plants that produce pine cone–shaped buds filled with aromatic resins, oils, and acids used for giving beer that yummy bitterness. Hops produce tannins that give beer a dry mouthfeel and finish, and also act as a natural preservative.
- **Yeast** is the ingredient that converts the grain sugars into alcohol, producing carbon dioxide—the bubbles or effervescence in your glass—in the process. This ingredient can either be top-fermenting, meaning it rises to the top during fermentation, as with ales, or bottom-fermenting, meaning it sinks to the bottom, as with lagers. Each type will lend your beer cocktail its own unique taste and texture.

Ale and Lager. All beer is split into two main types: Ale and lager. Ale is made with top-fermenting yeast and typically matures in a shorter amount of time (as little as seven days) because it is done at higher temperatures than lager. The shorter fermentation time means ale is less carbonated, cloudier, and has a higher alcohol content than lager. In general, ales have complex aromas and stylistically are fruitier, more acidic, and can be fuller-bodied, as in the case of stout. Of the two types, ale is more in your face and assertive.

Here are some common subcategories of ale you might find while out shopping:

Premium Bitter: This ale has a strong, hoppy flavor and is often called an ESB (Extra Strong Bitter Ale). Popular pours include Fuller's ESB, Redhook ESB, and Bass Ale.

Wheat Beer: This type of beer is made with mostly wheat and it's light in both hops and flavor. This category can be cloudy, and usually has a subtle fruit finish. Hefeweizen is the Bavarian specialty.

Lambic: These fruity, Belgian wheat beers are very food-friendly, winelike beers. Lambics are commonly flavored with raspberry (*framboise*), cherry (*kreik*), or peach (*pêche*). True lambics only come from Belgium. They are fermented with wild yeast and locally sourced bacteria for a unique sour, pungent quality.

Stouts and Porters: These ales are made with highly roasted barley, giving them an almost black color. Porters tend to be a little lighter than stouts, and have toasted and chocolate flavors, like Smith's Taddy Porter. Stouts, like Guinness, have the same roasted flavors as porters, with added coffee or creamy malted elements.

Saison: This Belgian pale ale is usually very carbonated, fruity, and sometimes spicy. It comes in larger, winelike bottles and is sometimes called "farmhouse ale," because it is brewed during the colder, less-active months on the farm. Hill Farmstead's Ann is a great example of this category of beer.

Brown Ale: These reddish, dark brown English ales are nutty with softer hop flavors, like Newcastle Brown Ale.

Pale Ale: These light-colored ales have a high hop character, which makes them more bitter. A popular example is Sierra Nevada Pale Ale.

Lagers are fermented at cooler temperatures with bottom fermenting yeast and are aged for a longer period of time than ales. These are typically crisp, smooth, and more subtle in flavor and aroma. However, *bocks, dopplebocks* (double bocks), *dunkels,* and lagers like Mexico's Negro Modelo can be dark and rich.

Here are some common subcategories of lager you might find while out shopping:

Pilsner: This is the most popular beer style in the world. These are pale in color, and tend to be bitter. Popular pilsners include Coor's Light, Stella Artois, and Pilsner Urquell.

Bock: These range from gold and tawny to dark brown. They are rich and full-bodied with pronounced maltiness. La Trappe Bockbier and St. Nikolaus Bock Bier are two popular brands.

Double Bock: These are basically more intense bocks. They are darker in color and higher in alcohol and you'll see the word *doppelbock* on labels, like the popular Ayinger Celebrator Doppelbock.

Triple Bock: This is an amped up double bock, and almost black in color. They can be up to 18% alcohol. Sam Adams' Triple Bock is a popular American brand.

Steam Beer: This is a high-temperature brew with no cold stabilization, so it's basically a combination of an ale and a lager. Steam beers are full of toasty malty aromas and heady hops. They can be crisp and fully carbonated like a lager but also fuller bodied like an ale. Anchor Steam Brewing Company is the most popular of this type.

SPEAKEASY

Craft beer is one that is typically made in small batches by an independent brewery or brewer.

PARTY FAVOR

Did you know that 4000 years ago in Babylonia, it was common practice for a bride's father to supply his new son-in-law with all the mead (honey beer) he could drink for a month after the wedding? This was once called the honey month, or as we know it today, the honeymoon.

Ginger Beer vs. Ginger Ale

Many cocktails call for ginger beer, but ginger beer isn't beer in the sense of ale and lager. Labeled "beer" because it is brewed and fermented, ginger beer is a primarily non-alcoholic beverage. Although it once contained traces of alcohol, these days the only kick you'll get from ginger beer is from its intense fresh ginger flavor. By contrast, ginger ale is a sweet, carbonated soda made from water and ginger, and lacks the spice and kick of fresh ginger in ginger beer.

❧ Get Your Drink On! ☙

While some beer-tails are simple, featuring beer and only one other component, more complex beer cocktails use beer as an ingredient rather than the main event. The drinks this month include both beer and ginger beer. If you stick with high-quality spirits, fresh ingredients, and keep an open mind about new flavor combinations, you're soon to find out that even beer-tails can be enlightening. Go ahead and get your drink on!

Tips for This Month

This month, setup is simple—just grab your bottle openers and pint glasses and you're good to go!

Pour in Stages

When pouring beer, you should hold the glass at a 45-degree angle and fill it only two-thirds full. Then straighten the glass and fill it to 1 inch (2.5 cm) from the top. Just as when pouring champagne, the carbonation will create a foamy top—called the head—that can continue to grow once you've stopped pouring. So pouring in stages prevents your beer from ending up on the table and instead stays in your glass.

Skip the Shaker

This cocktail club the rules have changed: No shaking. Beer comes carbonated and shaking may result in explosive cocktails! Drinks with larger amounts of brew only require a stir instead of a vigorous shake.

❧ Mainly Beer-Tails ☙

BEERMOSA

SERVES 1

Perfect for brunch, this easy beer-tail can be made by combining any wheat beer or light lager with orange juice, but I prefer a good mango or blood orange version.

For mango:
    1 cup (240 ml) wheat beer, chilled   *1 cup (240 ml) mango nectar, chilled*

For blood orange:
    1 cup (240 ml) freshly squeezed blood   *1 cup (240 ml) light lager (such as Peroni*
    orange juice, chilled   *Nastro Azzuro), chilled*

In a chilled pint glass, combine the ingredients and stir. If you are feeling more lady like, add 1 ounce of the fruit juice or nectar to a champagne flute and top with the wheat beer or light lager.

SHANDY LANE

Shandies are popular summer sips in London, and are made by mixing beer with citrus soda, carbonated lemonade, or plain lemonade. These drinks can be fruity, spicy, or even stiff, depending on what you mix into your pour.

Traditional Lemon Shandy

SERVES 1

1 cup (240 ml) lemonade, chilled   *1 cup (240 ml) lager, chilled*

Fill a tall chilled pint glass with the lemonade and top it with the lager. Make it raspberry by using raspberry lemonade in place of the regular lemonade, and throw in a few fresh raspberries for garnish.

Apricot Shandy

SERVES 1

1½ tablespoons sugar   *1 fresh apricot, sliced*
1 tablespoon freshly squeezed lemon juice   *1½ cups (240 ml) hefeweizen, chilled*

In a chilled pint glass, muddle together the sugar and lemon juice until all of the sugar is dissolved. Add about two-thirds of the apricot and lightly muddle it. Pour in the beer and stir to combine. Serve it with an apricot wedge or two as a garnish.

Pineapple Shandy

SERVES 1

4 to 6 fresh pineapple sage or sage leaves   *¾ cup (180 ml) mild lager, chilled (Red*
Ice cubes   *Stripe or Session Lager work great)*
¾ cup (180 ml) pineapple juice   *1 piece fresh pineapple, for garnish*

In a pint glass, lightly muddle the sage and add about 1 cup (240 ml) ice. Add the juice, top with the lager, and stir. Garnish with the pineapple.

Michelada, opposite

MICHELADA

This beer-tail takes the cake at our house in the summer. It's a cold *cerveza* (beer) with some spices or hot sauce and a squirt of fresh lime juice, served in a salt-rimmed pint glass. Sometimes they are made with tomato juice, clam juice, or Clamato (which is a mix of both), but this is my preferred version.

2 lime wedges
Coarse salt, for rimming the glass
1 teaspoon Frank's hot sauce (or substitute your favorite)

½ teaspoon Maggi seasoning or Worcestershire sauce
Ice cubes
1(12-ounce/360-ml) bottle Corona, chilled

Wet the rim of a chilled pint glass with a lime wedge and dip it in the salt. Add the hot sauce and Maggi and stir.

Fill the glass with ice. Pour in the chilled Corona. Stir and serve with the other lime wedge as garnish.

SHAKE IT UP

Serve it Frozen: On a hot summer day, I love to throw these in the blender. 2 cups (480 ml) of ice along with the ingredients above make for a delicious slushy drink to cool you down.

Add Some Spice: Add a pinch of smoked paprika and a pinch of cayenne. Serve with half a jalapeño on a skewer if you dare.

Make it Dark: Use a Negro Modelo (a dark Mexican beer) and add 2 teaspoons adobo sauce in place of Frank's and 1 teaspoon soy sauce in place of the Maggi.

Ginger Beer-Tails

MOSCOW MULE

SERVES 1

There is a small copper mug especially for serving this drink. If you don't own one, a simple pint glass will suffice.

½ lime
Ice cubes

¼ cup (60 ml) vodka
½ cup (120 ml) ginger beer, chilled

Squeeze the lime into a tall glass filled with ice. Drop the lime into the glass. Add the vodka, fill it with the ginger beer, and stir.

From left: Michelada and Kentucky Ginger, page 141 and below

KENTUCKY GINGER

SERVES 1

¼ cup (60 ml) bourbon
1 ounce ginger beer
2 dashes of Angostura bitters

Ice cubes
1 sprig fresh rosemary
1 piece candied ginger

Combine the bourbon, ginger beer, and bitters in a shaker filled with ice. Stir until they are well chilled and strain them into an empty glass.

Spoon the ice from the shaker into the glass. Garnish with the rosemary and make a cut about three-quarters of the way into the piece of candied ginger to hang it on the rim of the glass for a garnish.

Eat Up!

There's lots of grub that goes great with beer. Embracing the more casual vibe these drinks create, this month we're pairing our spicy Micheladas (page 141) with suitable mates like sweet potato wedges and sriracha ketchup. Serve up your favorite Shandy (page 139) with my fish and chips makeover, and last, but not least, the Bacon, Beer, and Barbecue Sliders (page 144) are awesome with any of our ginger beer-tails. Bon appetit!

CRISPY TILAPIA WITH HOMEMADE TARTAR AND SWEET CHILI SAUCES

SERVES 10 TO 12

For the sweet chili dipping sauce:
1 cup (100 g) sugar
½ cup (120 ml) rice wine vinegar
1 tablespoon sriracha (garlic-chile sauce available in the Asian section of your local market or at specialty Asian markets)
½ teaspoon red pepper flakes

For the fish:
¼ cup (30 g) all-purpose flour
Salt and fresh ground pepper
1 large egg, beaten with a splash of water
2 cups (230 g) panko-style bread crumbs
1 tablespoon lemon zest
1 pound (455 g) tilapia fillets, cut into strips 3½ to 4 inches (9 to 10 cm) long and ¾ inch (2 cm) thick
1 teaspoon Old Bay seasoning
Cooking spray

For the tartar sauce:
½ cup (120 ml) mayonnaise
2 tablespoons chopped capers
1 tablespoon freshly squeezed lemon juice
¾ teaspoon lemon zest
A few dashes of hot sauce
A few dashes of Worcestershire sauce
Salt and fresh ground pepper

Chopped fresh parsley, for garnish

2 lemons, cut into small wedges

Make the sweet chili sauce: In a small pot, combine the sugar, vinegar, and ½ cup (120 ml) of water and bring them to a boil. Transfer the sauce to a heatproof container to cool completely. Once it is cooled, add the sriracha and red pepper flakes and combine well. Store the sauce covered at room temperature or refrigerate it if making ahead.

Make the fish: Preheat the oven to 450°F (230°C). Set up three shallow dishes for dredging the fish: Place the flour in the first dish and season it with a little salt and pepper. Place the beaten egg and water in the second dish. Combine the panko and lemon zest in the third.

Season the fish with the Old Bay. Place a baking sheet in the hot oven to heat up while you bread the fish. Dip each fish strip in the flour, shaking off the excess, then in the egg, then evenly coat it with the panko and zest mixture. Once all the fish is breaded, remove the hot baking sheet and coat it with cooking spray. Place the breaded fish in an even layer on the baking sheet and bake it for about 8 to 10 minutes, flipping the pieces halfway through, or until the fish is cooked through and beginning to brown.

Make the tartar sauce: In a small bowl, combine the mayonnaise, capers, lemon juice, zest, hot sauce, and Worcestershire. Season with salt and pepper. Refrigerate until ready to serve.

Serve the fish warm with the tartar and sweet chili sauces, lemon wedges, and a sprinkle of fresh parsley.

SPICED SWEET POTATO WEDGES
WITH SRIRACHA KETCHUP

1 tablespoon olive oil
1 teaspoon chili powder
1 teaspoon ground cumin
½ teaspoon salt
¼ teaspoon fresh ground pepper

1 pound (455 g) sweet potatoes, cut into
 ¾-inch (2-cm) thick wedges, or
 1 (16 ounce/455 g) package frozen
 sweet potato wedges
½ cup (120 ml) ketchup
2 teaspoons sriracha

Preheat the oven to 425°F (220°C). In a large bowl, combine the oil, chili powder, cumin, salt, and pepper. Add the sweet potato wedges and toss until they are evenly coated. Arrange them in a single layer on a baking sheet. Bake the potatoes for 18 to 20 minutes, or until they are tender and beginning to brown, flipping them halfway through the cooking time. In a small bowl, combine the ketchup and sriracha. Serve the potato wedges warm with the sriracha ketchup.

BACON, BEER, AND BARBECUE SLIDERS

SERVES 12 TO 14

1 (3½- to 4-pound/1.6- to 1.8-kg) beef
 brisket, fat trimmed (not corned)
Salt and fresh ground pepper
1 teaspoon chili powder
1 tablespoon vegetable oil
1 large onion, sliced
¾ cup (180 ml) stout, like Guinness

¾ cup (180 ml) barbecue sauce (your own
 or store-bought)
4 cloves garlic, smashed
6 slices bacon, cooked, drained, and
 chopped
12 to 14 slider buns
1 cup (225 g) sliced pickled jalapeños
 (optional)

Season the brisket with salt, pepper, and the chili powder. In a large pan over medium-high heat (cast iron preferred), heat the oil. Add the brisket and brown it on all sides. In a Crock-Pot set to low, layer the onions across the bottom. Place the brisket on top.

Combine the stout, barbecue sauce, and garlic in a bowl. Pour them over the brisket. Add the bacon. Place the lid on and cook for it 8 to 10 hours (depending on size), occasionally basting the brisket with the sauce. Cook the brisket longer to shred it and shorter if you want to slice it. Place a scoop of shredded brisket or a couple of slices on each slider bun. Top each with extra sauce and pickled jalapeños, if you like, and serve.

10-Minute Happy Hour

Mix up a nice cold Michelada (page 141) and enjoy alongside some fresh guacamole. In a medium bowl, mash 3 avocados, add some chopped jalapeño, minced red onion, chopped tomatoes, throw in some hot sauce, squeeze in some fresh lime juice, and season with salt. Serve with chips for a perfectly chill happy hour in 10-minutes' time.

Suppressor #2, page 155

NOVEMBER

chapter 11

LIQUEURS & OTHER SPIRITS

The Supporting Cast

Beautiful bottles lining the back bar at the world's finest drinking establishments contain all sorts of spirits and liqueurs ranging from bitter to syrupy sweet. While liqueurs are not ideal on their own, a splash here and a dash there can transform dull drinks into sophisticated layered cocktails. It's time to find out which of these unique pours you'd like to make a mainstay in your stash. After this cocktail club, next time you belly up to the bar, you'll be fully prepared to order way beyond the basics.

Before & After

Many of the spirits we'll discuss this month fall into the category of aperitif or digestif, and some qualify as both.

An aperitif is a drink usually enjoyed before a meal. It's supposed to prime the palate, wake up your taste buds, and get them excited for the meal to come. Lots of low-alcohol pours work well as aperitifs, and some of the most popular include vermouth, Lillet, sparkling wine, or Campari.

A digestif is the exact opposite of an aperitif. These herbal or bitter drinks are meant for sipping after the meal to help you digest. Every European culture seems to have their preferred digestif. Holidays with my Italian in-laws aren't complete until the digestif tray is brought to the table—for them, the Italian Amaro Averna or a nip of sambuca are mainstays. Similarly, the French like to end their meals with pastis, and the Greeks' preferred digestif is a shot of ouzo.

Liqueur Up A liqueur is an alcoholic drink that is made with a distilled spirit (it can be a neutral grain spirit or a rum, tequila, or whiskey) that is flavored with any combination of fruits, herbs, spices, nuts, cream, and even flowers, and always includes added sugar. Liqueurs are typically sweet, though some are more bitter.

Seeing as there are hundreds of liqueurs and spirits in the marketplace, I've broken down the most popular pours on menus today by flavor profile—licorice and anise, fruity, bitter and herbal, nutty, and floral—into a comprehensive liqueur and spirits guide to help you decipher any cocktail menu out there.

Licorice and Anise

Absinthe, the most popular of the licorice-flavored liqueurs, has gotten a bad reputation over the years for allegedly causing addiction and hallucinations so real they may have even spurred a famous Swiss murder in 1905. Claims like this, due to an early lack of production regulations, were enough to have the drink prohibited in the U.S. for almost ninety years. Alas, the green fairy is back, and due to new regulations, no psycho-tropic effects have been reported since its rerelease. This potent, anise-flavored sip gets its herbal and medicinal flavors from a mix of botanicals including anise, fennel, and the very bitter herb wormwood (if herbal drinks aren't your thing, this is not your go-to cup). Unlike the vintage posters that portrayed it as a fluorescent green pour, absinthe is typically less neon and more of a grassy green, ranging from yellowish/lightly green-tinged to clear. We got a little taste of absinthe with the Sazerac (page 78), but in this month's Taste Test on page 151, we'll try it the traditional way with a sugar cube, water, and fancy slotted spoon (if you've got one).

If you like the taste of licorice in your glass, here are a few other popular options you may encounter while browsing the shelves of your liquor store:

- Ouzo
- Pastis
- Anisette
- Sambuca
- Arak
- Jägermeister
- Galliano
- Herbsaint

Feeling Fruity

Limoncello is one of the most popular fruity liqueurs, and nondescript bottles of this high-octane lemony Italian digestif sit behind every bar in Rome. Although my favorite limoncello-infused night involved a jazz bar and a fuzzy memory of a carousel ride, my advice is to be very wary of those neon yellow bottles—who knows what they put into those house blends. Instead, why don't you make your own?

HOW TO MAKE LIMONCELLO
MAKES 6 CUPS (1.4 ML)

The pith is the white part between the lemon rind and the flesh of the fruit. It's very bitter, so be sure to use a nice sharp paring knife to remove the peel, being careful not to include the pith. The fruit can be juiced and made into a lemon simple syrup or lemonade.

10 lemons, washed thoroughly and peeled, no pith

1 (750-ml) bottle vodka
2 cups (500 g) sugar

Place the lemon peels in a large container that has a lid. Pour the vodka over them. Cover the container and place it in a dark cool space for 10 days to 2 weeks. No need to stir or check on this. After the desired amount of steeping, strain the liquid through a fine-mesh strainer.

Combine 3 cups (720 ml) of water and the sugar in a pot over medium heat and stir until the sugar has dissolved. Let this simple syrup cool completely.

Once it is cool, add the syrup to the lemon vodka and stir to combine. Pour it into clean bottles and store it in the refrigerator or freezer until ready to enjoy.

Not a fan of lemon? Here are some other fruity liqueurs to add to your cocktails:

- **Orange:** Curaçao, Grand Marnier, triple sec, Cointreau, Mathilde orange liqueur, Gran Torres
- **Cherry:** Cherry Heering or Luxardo maraschino liqueur
- **Melon:** Midori
- **Citrus combined with Vanilla:** Licor 43 or Tuaca
- **Pomegranate:** PAMA liqueur, which is also excellent for making your own grenadine (see page 15).
- **Raspberry:** Chambord
- **Peach/Apricot:** Southern Comfort/Marie Brizzard's Apry
- **Apple:** Berentzen

The Herbal & Bitter Bunch

This category has both bitter and herbal sips included, giving us a nice mix of liqueurs that are a little on the medicinal side in the best way possible. Pimm's, a popular British brand of liqueurs, originally developed a series of seven bottled English cocktails based on different spirits: gin, whiskey, brandy, rum, rye, vodka, and tequila. Pimm's #1 Cup, the only one available in the United States currently, is based on gin and has citrusy, spicy, and bitter notes. In England, it's wildly popular as a summer drink mixed with their version of lemonade, which is more like American lemon-lime soda or ginger ale. As boozy lore would have it, there are only six people said to know the secret mix of herbs used to brew Pimm's #1 Cup.

A "cup" is another term for a British punch traditionally served to hunting parties in England before the hunters went off in search of their prize. Today, the cup has eased into garden parties, croquet, sporting events, and picnics at the governor's mansion. Feeling posh? Pour up a Pimm's #1 Cup (page 152).

If you find yourself continually reaching for more bitter pours, here are some other types to sip:

- Aperol: An orange-flavored (and colored) Italian pour that's excellent when mixed with Prosecco in the Aperol Fizz (page 166).
- Cynar: This Italian bittersweet drink comes from artichokes, and is often used with club soda to cure an upset stomach.
- Campari: We saw this liqueur make an appearance in the beloved Negroni (page 27). The iconic bitter, red-colored Italian liqueur is lower in alcohol, making the Campari and soda a perfect aperitif if you know you've got a long night ahead of you.
- Lillet: This French aperitif is made with wine and citrus, including orange peels, and a liqueur. It's often enjoyed alone, but it's equally delicious mixed up in a cocktail, like this month's Corpse Reviver #2 (page 156). You may find Lillet Blanc (white wine) or Lillet Rouge (red wine) when out shopping.
- Punt e Mes: This is a bold, bitter red vermouth that can be used in place of softer, more traditional red vermouths in cocktails like the Manhattan (page 77) or Negroni (page 27).
- Dubonnet: This French wine-based aperitif comes in red (Dubonnet Rouge—on the sweeter, richer side) or white (Dubonnet blanc), and includes a mix of herbs and spices and a touch of quinine (the same ingredient in tonic). It's not quite as bitter as some in this category, but it's still got a bite.
- Cocchi Americano: This Italian aperitif wine is similar to Lillet Blanc and vermouth, but sweeter, a little spicier, and a tad more bitter. This month we'll see it appear in the Corpse Reviver #2 (page 156).
- Bénédictine: This syrupy sweet liqueur has been around the block since 1510. Normandy monks used it to prevent malaria and eventually it went on to become popular when mixed with brandy (so much so that the company began bottling them together as B&B).
- Fernet Branca: This bitter drink has seen a popularity explosion of late among bartenders, servers, and cooks, earning it the nickname "hipster Jager" (short for Jägermeister). The Fernet trend started in San Francisco, where it's most often coupled with ginger ale or ginger beer. This is also a type of bitter Amaro (see below).
- Amaro: This is a category of Italian bittersweet herbal liqueurs that are made from a mixture of herbs, flowers, bark, roots, citrus peels, and spices. These are often thick and syrupy sweet (though still bitter), and are usually consumed as a digestif. Brands

PARTY FAVOR

Bitters like Fernet Branca are used as digestifs or hangover helpers.

include Averna, Nonino, and the cult favorite—Fernet Branca. Other types include Branca Menta (Fernet Branca blended with crème de menthe), which is very minty, and Zucca, which is rhubarb-based.

- Drambuie: This is a whiskey-based liqueur flavored with honey and spices.
- Chartreuse: This digestif comes in yellow or green. The yellow is milder and sweeter, but both are herbal and said to be made from a secret recipe including 130 herbs. Both Chartreuse styles are spicy, with all sorts of flavors such as cinnamon, cloves, and pine. Like many in the category, this has been believed to have medicinal qualities including aiding digestion and warding off sickness.

Nuts for Nuts: These sips have predominantly nutty characteristics. If you like pistachios in your ice cream and almonds for a midday snack, these sweet liqueurs will be right up your alley.

- Amaretto: A sweet sip made from almonds and apricots.
- Frangelico: A hazelnut liqueur.

Taste Test

While technically not cocktails served solo, there are two important herbal/bitter spirits you should explore this month. Think you're ready to play with the big boys at the bar? Then pour up a sip of the current bartender's cult pick—Fernet Branca. A straight shot is the go-to, but feel free to chill it or enjoy it on the rocks.

Next, pour a nip of another intense liqueur—absinthe. Get a bowl of sugar cubes, borrow or buy an absinthe spoon, and have your guests get familiar with the green fairy. To serve absinthe, fill your glass with a few ounces of the green liqueur and place one or two sugar cubes on a flat, slotted absinthe spoon balanced on top of your glass. Slowly pour water over top of the sugar cube and watch the green drink turn white.

Sip the two liqueurs side by side and discuss the differences. Both are medicinal and bitter, but do you like the addition of a sugar cube? Or do you prefer your bitter sips sans sugar?

Flower Power: Getting the garden into your glass is easy with these floral spirits. Mixing these into cocktails lends romantic perfume-y and sweet notes perfect for balancing the more abrasive ingredients you may be mixing up.

- St. Germain Elderflower Liqueur: This 40 proof artisanal liqueur is made from hand picked elderflowers, balanced by citrus notes and flavors of pear and lychee.
- Orange Flower Water: This spirit is distilled from orange blossoms and typically only a drop or two is added to the glass.

SPEAKEASY

Liqueurs labeled "crème de" are sweet liqueurs that don't actually contain cream at all. The "crème" refers to their creamy, thick consistency.

Get Your Drink On!

I've been looking forward to this month's cocktail club all year long because all of these liqueurs and ingredients make for very interesting drinks. Choose between the two Pimm's cocktails—either the classic, refreshing Pimm's #1 Cup (below) or the adventurous Suppressor #2 (page 155)—and mix up The Bijou (page 154) featuring the herbal Chartreuse, the classic Americano Highball (page 154) highlighting the bitter sip Campari, and the most popular of the Corpse Revivers, # 2 (page 156), featuring the aperitif Lillet Blanc. Grab your shakers—you're in for a very adventurous cocktail club!

Suppressor #2, page 155

Tips for This Month

This month, most of our liqueur-driven cocktails can be served in either coupe-style glasses or highballs.

The Classics

PIMM'S #1 CUP

SERVES 1

Also known as the Wimbledon Cooler, this drink may be served with apples, strawberries, rhubarb, lemon slices, rosemary, or mint sprigs. In fact, I've seen it served more as a fruit salad than a cocktail. If you're hungry, feel free to beef up the garnish, but if you'd just prefer to sip the cocktail, the simple cucumber garnish gets the job done.

Ice cubes
1½ ounces Pimm's #1
¼ cup (60 ml) lemon-lime soda (see Note)
1 ounce club soda
1 English cucumber spear, for garnish

SHAKE IT UP

For a different twist, try swapping the lemon-lime soda for Champagne and you've got a Royal Cup to toast with instead.

In a glass filled with ice, combine the Pimm's and sodas and stir. Garnish with the cucumber and serve.

Note: The original recipe calls for lemon-lime soda, but since American sodas tend to be sweeter, I like to cut mine with some club soda. You may also substitute lemonade or 1 ounce of fresh lemon juice and ginger ale.

THE BIJOU (JEWEL)

SERVES 1

Bijou is French for "jewel" and this drink gets that name because it mixes the colors of three jewels: diamonds (the crystal clear gin), rubies (the red vermouth), and emeralds (the Chartreuse).

Ice cubes
3 ounces (90 ml) gin
1 ounce (10 ml) green Chartreuse

1 ounce (10 ml) sweet vermouth
1 dash of orange bitters
Lemon peel, for garnish

In a shaker filled with ice, combine the gin, Chartreuse, vermouth, and bitters. Stir and strain them into a glass. Add the lemon peel for garnish.

THE AMERICANO HIGHBALL

SERVES 1

Ice cubes
1½ ounces sweet vermouth
1½ ounces Campari

Club soda
Flamed orange peel (see page 51)

In a tall glass filled with ice, add the vermouth, Campari, and top with club soda. Light your orange peel over your glass and drop it in for garnish.

❧ New Twists ☙

LIMONCELLO PROSECCO FLOAT

SERVES 1

Sgroppino, the Italian delight made with lemon sorbet, vodka, and Prosecco, inspired this cocktail. This one uses Limoncello (see page 149) in place of the lemon sorbet and vodka.

¼ cup (60 ml) limoncello, straight from the freezer

¼ cup (60 ml) Prosecco, chilled

Pour the limoncello into a chilled martini glass. Float the chilled Prosecco on top.

SUPPRESSOR #2

SERVES 1

The Suppressor is a new family of cocktails concocted by a bunch of bartending friends-from Atlanta, Georgia. Suppressors are a mix of low-alcohol spirits, wine, fortified wines, or vermouth. These lower-alcohol sips were created so that you can enjoy one, maybe even two midday, without needing a nap.

Ice cubes
1 ounce Pimm's #1
1 ounce Cocchi Americano or Lillet Blanc
1 tablespoon Dolin dry vermouth
1 tablespoon Zucca

1 dash of lemon bitters, such as Bitter
  Truths Lemon Bitters
1 lemon twist
3 thin cucumber slices
Sea salt

In a shaker filled with ice, combine the Pimm's, Cocchi Americano, vermouth, Zucca, and bitters. Shake and strain them into a glass.

Express the lemon oils from the skin of the lemon into the drink and discard the lemon twist. Top the Suppresor with the cucumber slices and a pinch of sea salt.

Recipe courtesy of Miles Macquerrie, Leon's Full Service, Decatur, Georgia.

THE CORPSE REVIVER #2

SERVES 1

Where Suppressors are meant to be lower-alcohol sips, on the other side of this movement stands traditional cocktails called "corpse revivers." These drinks are designed to revive the body after a night of drinking. The *Savoy Cocktail Book* states they are, "To be taken before 11 a.m., or whenever steam and energy are needed."

Ice cubes
1 ounce gin
1 ounce Cointreau
1 ounce Lillet Blanc

1 ounce freshly squeezed lemon juice
1 dash of absinthe
1 orange twist, for garnish

In a shaker filled with ice, combine the gin, Cointreau, Lillet, lemon juice, and absinthe. Shake until well chilled and strain them into a chilled glass. Express the orange peel, drop it in the glass, and enjoy.

Eat Up!

So many flavors, so little time! This month, our drinks bring loads of personality to the table so our snacks of curried cauliflower and an assortment of grilled cheeses are versatile enough to go with many of them. Be playful with your pairings and see which you like best.

MINI GRILLED CHEESE SANDWICHES

SERVES 12

¼ cup (½ stick/55 g) unsalted butter,
   softened
4 slices sourdough bread

4 slices rye bread
4 ounces (115 g) Gruyère cheese, sliced
4 ounces (115 g) smoked Gouda, sliced

Heat a nonstick sauté or griddle pan over medium heat. Spread ½ tablespoon of the butter on one side of each slice of bread. Place 2 slices of rye bread, butter-side down, into the pan. Top each slice with 2 ounces each Gruyère and top with the other 2 slices of rye, butter-side up. Cook until the sandwiches are golden and the cheese is melted, about 2 minutes per side. Repeat with the sourdough and smoked Gouda.

Let the sandwiches cool for just a few minutes before slicing them into 1- to 1½-inch-thick (2.5- to 4-cm) strips. Serve them warm or at room temperature.

ROASTED CURRIED CAULIFLOWER WITH RAITA

SERVES 8 TO 12

For the cauliflower:
- 3 tablespoons olive oil
- 1 tablespoon plus 1 teaspoon yellow curry powder
- 1 teaspoon ground cumin
- ¼ teaspoon red pepper flakes
- ½ teaspoon salt
- About 8 cups (1,820 g) cauliflower florets

For the raita:
- ½ cup (120 ml) plain Greek-style yogurt
- 1 clove garlic, minced
- ½ cup (115 g) shredded cucumber
- 1 tablespoon chopped fresh mint
- Pinch of salt
- Few grinds of fresh ground pepper

Make the cauliflower: Preheat the oven to 425°F (220°C). In a large bowl, combine the oil and spices. Add the cauliflower and toss well until it is evenly coated with the oil and spice mixture. Spread the florets in an even layer on a rimmed baking sheet and roast them for 20 to 25 minutes, or until the cauliflower is tender and beginning to brown.

Make the raita: In a medium bowl, combine all of the ingredients and refrigerate them until ready to serve.

Serve the cauliflower warm or at room temperature with the raita.

10-Minute Happy Hour

It'd be a shame to have to shorten cocktail club this month, but if you had to just pick one sip for this month's 10-minute happy hour, I suggest you make it the Suppressor #2 (page 155). It's filled with several liqueurs we discussed this month, including the famous Pimm's #1. Serve it alongside some fresh sliced cucumbers and hummus for a tasty happy hour.

Kir Royale, page 164

DECEMBER
chapter 12

BUBBLY COCKTAILS

Drinking the Stars

You did it—a full year of mixing up cocktails with your friends and drinking outside your comfort zone! By now, you've gotten familiar with the main spirit categories, cozied up to your cocktail shaker, and you're all set to navigate any cocktail menu that comes your way. So this month, we're breaking out the bubbly to mix up a few more drinks to toast your cocktail club success. Pop those corks and prepare to be drenched in all things bubbly.

Get to Know Your Bubbles

Really, how much do you need to know to enjoy Champagne? Not a lot, that's for sure—you've probably already raised a glass or two in your life, and had a fine old time with it. But if you're ready to delve a little deeper and mix up these bubbles in cocktails, then here's a crash course.

Any wine that sparkles can be called sparkling wine, but not all wine that sparkles can be called Champagne. Technically, the name Champagne is only given to sparkling wine hailing from the Champagne region in the northeast of France. Bubbly from anywhere else on the globe is sparkling wine and certain regions use different monikers, including:

- *France:* Vin mousseux, Cremant d' Alsace, or Cremant d' Bourgogne
- *Spain:* Cava
- *Italy:* Prosecco, Spumante, and Frizzante
- *Germany:* Sekt

Taste Test

As always, the best way to learn about these different sparklers is to taste them. So before you mix them all into cocktails this month, place a 1-ounce pour of Champagne, Prosecco, Cava, and a sparkler from California side by side for your cocktail club to see, sniff, and taste the differences.

You Can Judge a Bottle by Its Label

When it comes to sparkling wine, there is usually a lot on the label that will help you decipher what's inside. Here are a few terms to keep an eye out for:

Blanc de Blanc: This term literally means "white from white," and refers to white Champagne made from Chardonnay, a white grape.

Blanc de Noir: This term literally means "white from black," and refers to white Champagne made from Pinot Noir, a red grape. Though made solely from red grapes, this bubbly can range in color from slightly pink to clear.

Rosé: If you see "Rosé" on a bubbly's label, what's inside will range from salmon-colored to pink and sparkling. The pink hue of Rosé Champagne and sparkling Rosé is the result of grape skins coming into contact with the juice during fermentation. This can also be achieved by the actual addition of Rosé wine at the end of the winemaking process.

Doux or Dolce: This means "sweet" in French and Italian, respectively.

Demi-Sec: This literally means "half dry," which is still pretty sweet.

Extra-Dry or Extra-Sec: Though not as dry as brut, this sparkling wine is very dry, meaning it is not as sweet.

PARTY FAVOR

Champagne can only be made with these three grapes: Chardonnay, Pinot Noir, and Pinot Meunier. Outside of Champagne, all grapes are fair game when making bubbly wine.

Brut: This is really dry, and typically what we want when mixing cocktails. Ultra Brut, Extra Brut, or Natural are other variations of dry bubbly.

No Number Games

There is a lot of talk about a wine's vintage—the year when its grapes are harvested— because the weather in a particular growing season can have an effect on the wine in the bottle. However, most sparkling wines are nonvintage, or "NV." This means they're made of grapes harvested from a combination of years. The only time you'd see a vintage on a bottle of bubbly is if the producers felt they had a particularly exceptional year, and decided to bottle only grapes from that harvest. If that's the case, it is usually reflected in a hefty price tag.

HOMEMADE BRANDIED CHERRIES

MAKES ABOUT 4 CUPS (910 G)

Brandied cherries are a great garnish to have on your bar. They're simple to make and fun for swapping in any drink that calls for a maraschino cherry garnish, like a Manhattan or an Amaretto Sour, and simply dropping one or two into a flute of freshly poured bubbles makes for a delicious addition.

½ cup (100 g) sugar
2 teaspoons freshly squeezed lemon juice
1 cinnamon stick
1 star anise
½ vanilla bean

1 pound (455 g) fresh sweet cherries, washed, stemmed, and pitted
½ teaspoon vanilla extract
1 cup (240 ml) brandy

In a saucepan, combine ½ cup (120 ml) of water, the sugar, lemon juice, cinnamon stick, star anise, and vanilla bean. Bring them to a simmer and stir to dissolve the sugar. Add the cherries and simmer for 5 minutes. Remove the pan from the heat and add the vanilla extract and brandy. Stir.

Once the cherries have cooled, you may jar these or transfer them to a container with a fitted lid. Cover and refrigerate them for up to 6 months, if they last that long.

How to Give a Great Toast

With the holidays upon us, parties and celebrations start to polka dot the calendar. Whether you're the host or just an enthusiastic guest looking to raise a glass, 'tis the season for toasting. To keep your cocktail club toasts from turning the night sour, here are a few quick tips to making sure your toast is memorable, and more importantly, brief.

- It's not about you! Try to avoid giving a long-winded introduction of yourself.
- Be specific to the event or the person you are actually toasting. Using personal anecdotes will make the people you're toasting feel special.
- Make eye contact. In some cultures, avoiding eye contact is considered bad luck!
- Try not to memorize your toast, so your words sound genuine and not rehearsed. It's OK to use notes to help you along, but a sweet and imperfect story and a smile will mean more than an awkwardly rehearsed speech.
- Know your audience. Nothing kills momentum faster than making your audience uncomfortable.

- Keep it positive! Your toast is always best kept on a high note.
- Keep it brief. Aim for about a minute in length, then raise your glass to signal the end of the toast.

❦ Get Your Drink On! ❧

Bubbly on its own can range in color from clear to straw to salmon on to pink. When you look at a glass of bubbly also pay attention to the strands of bubbles—are they big or small? Are there a lot or just a few? In general, Italian and Spanish bubblies have bigger bubbles that are less assertive, while French and Californian styles maintain strong necklaces of delicate bubbles. All bubbly wine will be light-bodied unless you are sipping a dessert variety, which will be richer in mouthfeel. Some of the aromas you'll notice range from yeast or toast to citrus, pear, apples, and florals. Prosecco is known for peach and apricot scents while French and American pours lean towards yeasty and fruity aromas. Pink-hued bubblies, like blanc de noirs, can smell like pink fruits such as dried strawberries, ripe raspberries, and cherries.

When mixed in cocktails, the most important attribute of bubbly wine is the spritz. It can range from a slight fizz to an explosive party in your mouth. Note how the bubbles can change a finish. Not only will sparkling cocktails finish fresh and bright, they will also make your mouth water, leaving you wanting for more. While mimosas and bellinis are definitely famous bubbly cocktails, we'll be moving into more interesting territory for this month's tasting. Some vintage pours include the Champagne Cocktail (page 164), complete with a generous hit of bitters; the gin-based French 75 (opposite); and the classic Kir Royale (page 164). A new favorite of mine, the Sparkling Strawberry-Mint Smash (page 164), is pretty in pink but not a super sweet sip. If you're looking for a sweeter drink, wrap up this year of cocktail club with a farewell smooch From Russia with Love (page 164).

Tips for This Month

When it comes to mixing up Champagne cocktails, typically you don't need an expensive bottle of Dom Perignon or even a mid-range bottle of Veuve Cliquot, for that matter. The best bang for your buck is definitely Cava from Spain or a Prosecco from Italy. Most ring in under $20. To be authentic, I'd suggest you include Champagne for the Champagne Cocktail, the French 75, and the Kir Royale.

It's All in the Glass

You'll need both flutes and coupe glasses this month. The small mouth and long stem of a flute is perfect for keeping the bubbles from escaping sparkling wines and primarily bubbly-based sips, while the old-school beauty of the coupe is just darling for champagne cocktails.

How to Pop the Cork

Remember to always chill your sparkling wine, because otherwise it will explode upon opening. Keep these steps in mind when pulling the plug on a bottle of bubbly:

- Hold It! Grip the bottle with your weaker hand at the base and your stronger hand on top of the cork.
- Foil Off: Remove the foil and wire cage from around the cork carfully. Drape a clean kitchen towel or linen napkin over the exposed cork.
- Twist: Tilt the bottle away from you (and everyone else!) at a 45-degree angle. With the cloth still over the top of the bottle, grasp the cork with one hand and gently twist the bottle—not the cork—with the other. Let the pressure in the bottle gently force out the cork.

Pouring Primer

Start with a 1-ounce pour. This called "priming the glass." Let the bubbles settle, then finish pouring until the glass is about two-thirds full. If you are making a cocktail like the Aperol Fizz or the Elderflower Spritzer, those spirits act as the primer and there is no need to pour the bubbles in two steps.

The Classics

FRENCH 75

SERVES 1

This drink was named after a piece of artillery that was used during WWI and WWII.

Ice cubes
¼ cup (60 ml) gin
1 teaspoon simple syrup (page 15)

1 ounce freshly squeezed lemon juice
Champagne, chilled

In a cocktail shaker filled with ice, add the gin, syrup, and lemon juice. Shake to chill them. Strain the drink into a flute and top it with Champagne. You can also serve this in a Collins glass half full of ice.

CHAMPAGNE COCKTAIL

SERVES 1

1 sugar cube
4 to 6 dashes of Angostura bitters

Champagne, chilled
Lemon twist, for garnish

Drop the sugar cube into the bottom of a champagne flute. Coat the cube with the bitters and fill the glass with Champagne. Add the twist and enjoy.

KIR ROYALE

SERVES 1

At the Culinary Institute of America's famed Escoffier restaurant, this is the traditional French aperitif of choice.

1 tablespoon crème de cassis

3 ounces (90 ml) Champagne, chilled

In a champagne flute, add the crème de cassis and top it with the Champagne.

⁂ New Twists ⁂

SPARKLING STRAWBERRY-MINT SMASH

SERVES 1

3 to 4 fresh mint leaves
2 to 3 dashes of Angostura bitters
3 ripe strawberries, 2 hulled and sliced,
    and 1 left whole with stem

1 ounce Cognac
Sparkling Rosé, chilled

In a tall glass, add the mint (crumbling to bruise the leaves before dropping them in the glass) and the bitters. Lightly muddle them. Add the sliced strawberries and Cognac; muddle again lightly. Top with the Rosé, pour into a coupe glass, and garnish with the remaining whole strawberry.

FROM RUSSIA WITH LOVE

SERVES 1

1 tablespoon Godiva dark chocolate liqueur
1 tablespoon Chambord

Champagne, chilled
Cacao nibs, for garnish (optional)

In a champagne flute, add the Godiva and Chambord and top them with Champagne. Sprinkle on a couple of nibs if you like.

APEROL FIZZ

SERVES 1

The Aperol Fizz was the very first drink that started my cocktail club. We kicked off our monthly wine club with this darling orangey spritzer and from then on it was au revoir wine club and HELLO cocktail club! One sip and you'll see why.

1 ounce Aperol   *3 ounces (90 ml) Prosecco, chilled*

In a champagne flute, pour in the Aperol and top it with the Prosecco.

SHAKE IT UP

For an Elderflower Spritz, replace the Aperol with ½ to 1 ounce of elderflower liqueur and top with chilled bubbly.

❧ Eat Up! ❧

We have a wonderful assortment of nibbles perfect for this month's cocktail club or any holiday soiree you may be hosting. Mini crudités and an easy black truffle–infused bruschetta set the scene for a fabulous cocktail party, not to mention they are perfect paired with an Aperol Fizz (page 164) or a traditional Champagne Cocktail (page 164). The sweet bite of our Rosemary-Lemon Bars (opposite) is just as delicious alongside our sweeter bubbly cocktails this month.

RICOTTA, TRUFFLE OIL, & FRESH CRACKED PEPPER BRUSCHETTA

SERVES 10 TO 12

*1 baguette, about 22 inches (55 cm) long,
  sliced on the bias*
1 to 2 tablespoons olive oil
*15 ounces (430 g) part-skim ricotta,
  Sorrento is preferred*

Truffle oil, for drizzling
Fresh ground pepper
Sea salt

Preheat the broiler and position a rack 5 to 6 inches (12 to 15 cm) from the broiler. Place the baguette slices on a baking sheet and brush the tops with olive oil. Broil the bread until it is golden, about 2 to 3 minutes. (Times will vary as all broilers have different strengths. Keep an eye on them.)

166

CHAPTER 12

Top each toasted baguette slice with 1 tablespoon ricotta and drizzle it with truffle oil. Grind some pepper over each one and finish with a sprinkle of sea salt. Serve immediately.

MINI CRUDITÉS WITH HOMEMADE BLUE CHEESE DRESSING

SERVES 10 TO 12

For the blue cheese dressing:

½ cup (115 g) blue cheese crumbles
¼ cup (60 ml) buttermilk
¼ cup (60 ml) sour cream
1 tablespoon freshly squeezed lemon juice

2 tablespoons finely chopped fresh chives (optional)
½ teaspoon kosher salt
1 teaspoon fresh ground pepper

For the crudités

½ large red bell pepper, cut into 12 (3½- to 4-inch/9- to 10-cm) strips
½ large yellow pepper, cut into 12 (3½- to 4-inch/9- to 10-cm) strips
36 green beans, trimmed (about 8 ounces/225 g)

6 stalks celery, cut into 24 (3½- to 4-inch/9- to 10-cm) sticks
6 medium to large carrots, cut into 24 (3 ½- to 4-inch/9- to 10-cm) sticks

Make the dressing: In a bowl, whisk all the ingredients together until they are smooth and well combined.

Make the crudités: Fill 12 standard-size shot glasses (mine are 2 ounces/60 ml) with 2 teaspoons of the blue cheese dressing. Evenly divide the vegetables into each glass (3 green beans, 2 pieces each of the carrots and celery, and 1 of each type of pepper). Refrigerate until ready to serve.

Note: To substitute store-bought dressing, use 1 cup (240 ml).

ROSEMARY-LEMON BARS

SERVES 10 TO 12

For the crust:

½ cup (1 stick/115 g) unsalted butter, softened
¼ cup (50 g) granulated sugar

1 cup (130 g) all-purpose flour
Pinch of salt
1 tablespoon chopped fresh rosemary

For the filling:

1½ cups (300 g) granulated sugar
½ cup (120 ml) freshly squeezed lemon juice
½ cup (65 g) all-purpose flour

3 large eggs, at room temperature
1 tablespoon lemon zest
½ cup (50 g) powdered sugar for dusting

Preheat the oven to 350°F (175°C). Line an 8-by-8-inch (20-by-20-cm) baking dish with foil, letting some hang over the edge.

Make the crust: Using a stand mixer or hand mixer, beat together the butter and sugar until creamy. In a separate bowl, whisk together the flour and salt, then slowly add them to the butter mixture while blending on low. Once they are well combined, stir in the rosemary.

Pour the crust mixture into the prepared pan and press it down to form an even layer with some coming up the sides (you can use a flat-bottomed item like a measuring cup or ramekin to try and make it as even as possible). Refrigerate it for 10 minutes.

Remove the crust from the refrigerator and bake it until it barely begins to brown and looks slightly puffy, about 15 to 20 minutes. Remove it from the oven, leaving the oven on, and cool the crust on a rack while you make the filling.

Make the filling: In a medium bowl, whisk together the granulated sugar, lemon juice, flour, eggs, and zest until well combined. Pour them into the cooled crust and bake for 20 to 25 minutes, or until the bars are just barely jiggly in the center.

Allow the bars to cool in the pan for at least 1 hour before slicing. To slice, pull the bars out of the pan using the foil overhang and dust them with the powdered sugar. Cut them into 32 (½-inch/12-mm) squares and serve.

10-Minute Happy Hour

If you're looking to simplify this month, put some bubbly in the fridge and pick up a bottle of crème de cassis to serve a sparkler that is easy and elegant to pull off in no time. The Kir Royale (page 164) works great with almost any nibbles. Pick up a spinach and artichoke dip and serve it in a fresh sourdough boule or simply put out an assortment of traditional holiday sweets for guests to graze while you toast the holiday season.

Kir Royale, page 164

Resources

Bergeron, Victor Jules. *Trader Vic's Bartender's Guide*. New York: Doubleday, 1972.

Calabrese, Salvatore. *The Complete Home Bartender's Guide*. New York: Sterling Epicure, 2012.

Craddock, Harry. *The Savoy Cocktail Book*. London: Constable & Co., 1930.

Degroff, Dale. *Craft of the Cocktail*. New York: Clarkson Potter, 2002.

Haigh, Ted. *Vintage Spirits & Forgotten Cocktails*. Beverly, MA: Quarry Books, 2009.

Meehan, Jim, Chris Gall. *The PDT Cocktail Book*. New York: Sterling Epicure, 2011.

Parsons, Brad Thomas. *Bitters*. Berkeley: Ten Speed Press, 2011.

Regan, Gary. *The Joy of Mixology*. New York: Clarkson Potter, 2003.

Spivak, Mark. *Iconic Spirits*. Guilford, CT: Lyons Press, CT, 2012.

Wondrich, David. *Esquire Drinks*. New York: Hearst Books, 2004.

Wondrich, David. *Imbibe!* New York: Perigree, 2007.

Wondrich, David. *Punch*. New York: Perigree 2010.

www.imbibemagazine.com
www.sommelierjournal.com
www.gazregan.com
www.ajrathbun.com
www.alcademics.com
www.artofdrink.com
www.cocktailchronicles.com
www.cocktailians.com
www.drinkboy.com
www.jeffreymorgenthaler.com
http://drinks.seriouseats.com
www.thekitchn.com/drinks

Acknowledgments

To all of the people who helped bring this book to life: Thank you from the bottom of my heart.

Mom and Dad, it sounds cliché but it's the truth—I would not be here without you. Thanks for always encouraging me to be my best and for giving my boys the best Mimi and Rara in the world.

Michael, the perfect partner and my first editor, you make me want to be a better writer, and actually do with all your witty edits (though some unfit for print, they still make me laugh). Thanks for being a single dad while I hammered this out. You are still the hottest bartender I know. Christopher and Elliot, my ridiculously cute people: You inspire me everyday—thanks for the laughs and snuggles. Mommy loves you.

To my family, Coleen & Jerry, Dave & Christie, K & Sean, and the Petrosky clan, thanks for all of your love and support.

To my agent, Mel Flashman, thanks for allowing your love of American whiskey to drive the sale of this book. Please give the ever-poised Michael Ferrante a raise for fielding my unending phone calls. Thank you for your constant reassurance every step of the way.

I am indebted to the visionaries at Abrams. Topping that list are my fabulous, insightful, crazy smart, and creative editors: Leslie Stoker and Cristina Garces. I can't imagine any other writer has had it better than I. Thank you.

To the super cool and talented photo crew— Thayer Gowdy, Karen Schaupeter, Suzanne Lenzer, Philip Nondorf. You made this book gorgeous.

To Vanessa Parker McIntrye, for her recipe testing, culinary prowess, and mostly for being an amazing friend. To David Wondrich, Dale DeGroff, Lew Bryson, and Amy Zavatto for all your expert guidance. On that note, cheers to all of my friends in the trenches with me in this crazy biz.

To Alexandra Sklansky, Frank Coleman, and Lisa Harkins, and my boys at Beam, Dan Cohen and Clarkson Hine, and all of the members of the Distilled Spirits Council for helping me master the spirits scene.

To the team at the *TODAY* show: the rock star Adam J. Miller, the genius Tammy Fuller, the fab Joanne LaMarca, the amazing Rainy Farrell and Brittany Shrieber, and the best kitchen crew in TV: Bianca, Ali, Deb, and our departed but not forgotten Lish. To Hoda and Kathie Lee for living by the motto "It's five o'clock somewhere." I love hanging out with you two! Natalie, Al, Willie, Carson, and Savannah—thanks for tasting my drinks, eating my apps, and indulging in my ideas, all with genuine interest and a smile.

To Faith Durand, at thekitchn.com, for giving me a shot and making me get a new camera. The 10-Minute Happy Hour would not exist without you. To the rest of the ubertalented Kitchn team sprinkled across the globe, I'm so proud to be part of it.

Finally, to all of the die-hard *The Wine Club* fans, thanks for eight years of love and happy wine clubs. Now it's time to flip the switch, grab a shaker, and get your mixed drink on!

Index